LISTER

MASTERS OF ART

THE IMPRESSIONISTS

The origins of modern painting

FRANCESCO SALVI

◆

ILLUSTRATED BY
L.R. GALANTE, ANDREA RICCIARDI

PETER BEDRICK BOOKS

DoGi

Produced by
Donati-Giudici Associati, Florence
Original title:
Gli Impressionisti
Text
Francesco Salvi
Illustrations
L.R. Galante
Andrea Ricciardi
Editorial coordination
Francesco Fiorentino
Teresa Domenici
Francesca Romei
Art direction and design
Oliviero Ciriaci
Research
Francesca Donati
Editing
Enza Fontana
Pagination
Monica Macchiaioli
Desktop publishing
Ugo Micheli
English translation
Deborah Misuri-Charkham
Editor, English-language edition
Ruth Nason
Typesetting
Ken Alston – A.J. Latham Ltd

Published in the United States
by Peter Bedrick Books
A division of NTC/Contemporary
Publishing Group, Inc.
4255 West Touhy Avenue
Lincolnwood (Chicago)
Illinois 60712-1975 U.S.A.

Library of Congress
Cataloging-in-Publication Data
Salvi, Francesco.
The impressionists: the origin of
modern painting / Francesco Salvi;
illustrations by L.R. Galante, Andrea
Ricciardi.
[Impressionisti. English]
p. cm.—(Masters of Art)
Includes index.
ISBN 0-87226-314-2
1.Impressionism (Art)—History. 2.
Art, Modern—19th century—
History. 3. Art, Modern—20th
century—History.
N6465.I4 S2513 1994
759.05'4—dc20   94-16930   CIP

Printed in Italy by
Eurolitho spa
Cesano Boscone (Milan)

Photolitho:
Venanzoni DTP, Florence

Fourth Printing, 2000

◆ HOW TO READ THIS BOOK

ILLUSTRATED PAGES

Each double page is dedicated to a specific topic which is presented in the large, central illustration. The text at the top of the left-hand page explains the illustration, which is an accurate reconstruction of a place or important event. Further drawings, paintings, photographs and artifacts complete the picture. The text in italics is a chronological biography of the Impressionist group.

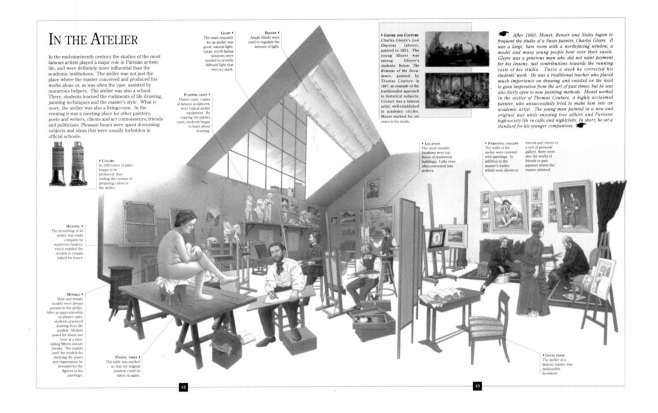

PAGES ABOUT THE ARTISTS

Pages 46-61 are dedicated to the eleven artists who made up the Impressionist group. Each section, on one artist, includes a biography (in the left-hand column), discussion of a great work (reproduced in the center of the page) and some analysis of its important details, an explanation of the particular significance of the artist's work and other examples of his or her paintings.

CONTENTS

THE CHARACTERS

During the second half of the nineteenth century in France, a group of artists revolutionized painting. Although they came from diverse backgrounds and differed in temperament and political beliefs, they shared a dissatisfaction with the prevailing artistic culture and were disappointed at their lack of success in official exhibitions. They were determined to establish a new method of painting. Their names were Edouard Manet, Claude Monet, Pierre Auguste Renoir, Edgar Degas, Paul Cézanne, Camille Pissarro, Alfred Sisley, Gustave Caillebotte, Berthe Morisot, Armand Guillaumin, and Mary Cassatt. Unlike the established French artists of the time, who painted mostly sacred, historical and mythological subjects, the group enjoyed depicting real-life, everyday scenes and landscapes. They preferred to work outdoors and used bright colors. They were more interested in painting shades of light than in precision drawing. Between 1850 and 1880 they worked mainly in Paris. In 1874 they held a joint exhibition. Afterwards, a journalist scornfully referred to them as "impressionists", meaning that their paintings were merely the representation of a first impression. The painters adopted this name for themselves and made history.

A COMMUNARD ✦
Early in 1871 the people took power in Paris and established a radical government. This regime was known as the "Commune".

A PRUSSIAN SOLDIER ✦
In 1870 Prussia defeated France, bringing an end to the Second Empire.

LOUIS ADOLPHE THIERS ✦
First President of the Third Republic, the regime which followed the fall of the Second Empire.

✦**PAUL DURAND-RUEL**
Born in Paris in 1831, he was an art dealer who met Monet and Pissarro in 1871. Through him the group's works gained esteem on the world market.

✦**THE HAVEMEYERS**
He was a banker, she an appraiser of the Impressionists. They brought the movement to the attention of the American market.

✦**FÉLIX NADAR**
Born in Paris in 1820, the greatest French photographer of the century. The group's first exhibition was held in his studio.

✦**GUSTAVE CAILLEBOTTE**
Wealthy naval engineer and eligible bachelor, he was the youngest in the group, born in Paris in 1848.

✦**ARMAND GUILLAUMIN**
A Parisian, born in 1841, and very poor until a lottery win permitted him to dedicate himself to painting.

✦**BERTHE MORISOT**
Born in Bourges in 1841, she soon moved to Paris. She was a cultured and sensitive painter.

MARY CASSATT ✦
Born in Pittsburgh in 1845, she arrived in Paris in 1866 and frequented high society.

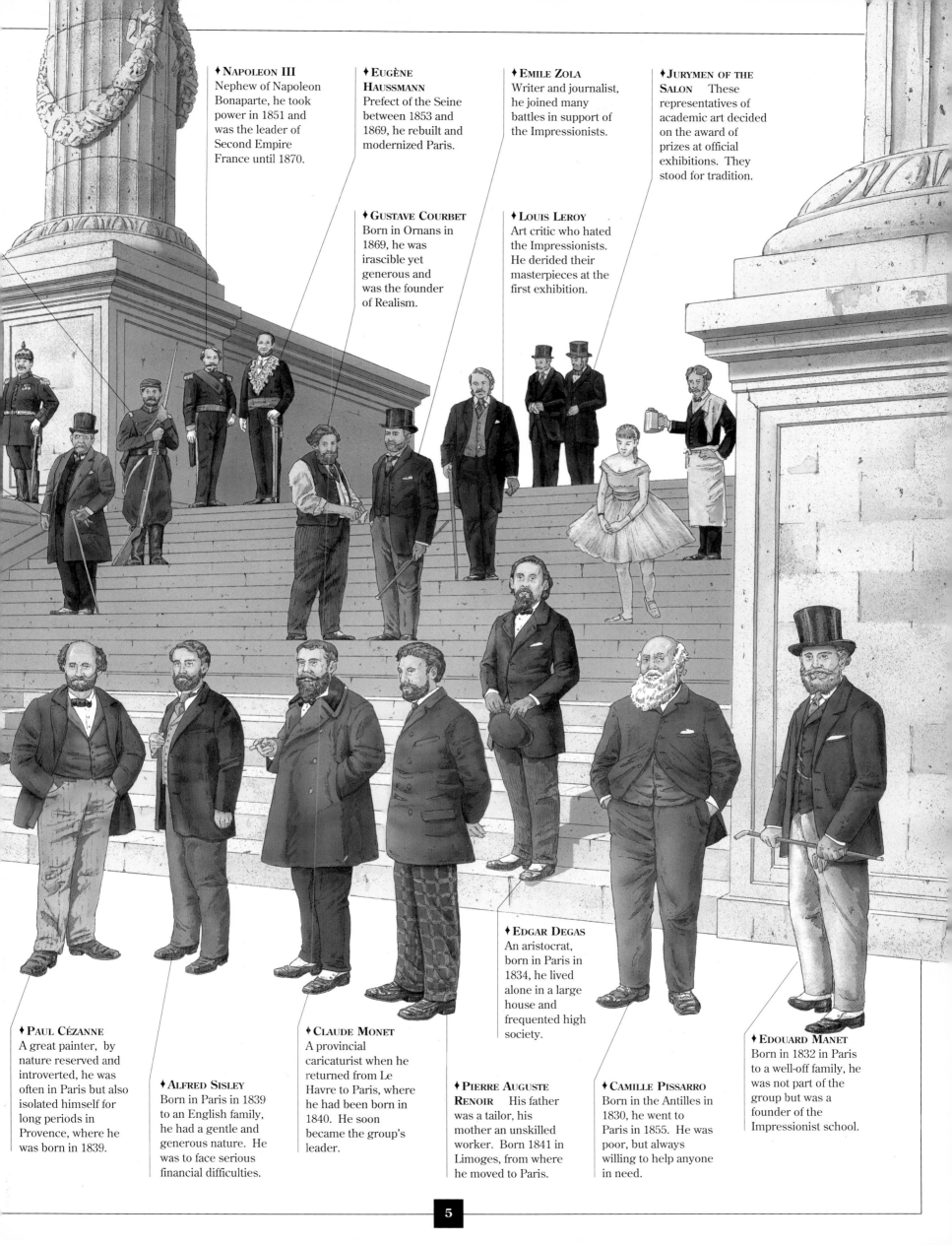

♦ **NAPOLEON III** Nephew of Napoleon Bonaparte, he took power in 1851 and was the leader of Second Empire France until 1870.

♦ **EUGÈNE HAUSSMANN** Prefect of the Seine between 1853 and 1869, he rebuilt and modernized Paris.

♦ **EMILE ZOLA** Writer and journalist, he joined many battles in support of the Impressionists.

♦ **JURYMEN OF THE SALON** These representatives of academic art decided on the award of prizes at official exhibitions. They stood for tradition.

♦ **GUSTAVE COURBET** Born in Ornans in 1869, he was irascible yet generous and was the founder of Realism.

♦ **LOUIS LEROY** Art critic who hated the Impressionists. He derided their masterpieces at the first exhibition.

♦ **PAUL CÉZANNE** A great painter, by nature reserved and introverted, he was often in Paris but also isolated himself for long periods in Provence, where he was born in 1839.

♦ **ALFRED SISLEY** Born in Paris in 1839 to an English family, he had a gentle and generous nature. He was to face serious financial difficulties.

♦ **CLAUDE MONET** A provincial caricaturist when he returned from Le Havre to Paris, where he had been born in 1840. He soon became the group's leader.

♦ **EDGAR DEGAS** An aristocrat, born in Paris in 1834, he lived alone in a large house and frequented high society.

♦ **PIERRE AUGUSTE RENOIR** His father was a tailor, his mother an unskilled worker. Born 1841 in Limoges, from where he moved to Paris.

♦ **CAMILLE PISSARRO** Born in the Antilles in 1830, he went to Paris in 1855. He was poor, but always willing to help anyone in need.

♦ **EDOUARD MANET** Born in 1832 in Paris to a well-off family, he was not part of the group but was a founder of the Impressionist school.

THE PLACES

The Impressionists' story takes place mainly in Paris which, together with London, was one of the most important European cities of the century. Their paintings were the first to portray life in a large, bourgeois metropolis and to depict how the poor worked and the rich enjoyed themselves. Their lives and paintings were based on districts of Paris: the Batignolles quarter where they had their studios, the bridges over the Seine, meeting places like the Moulin de la Galette, the Louvre where they studied art of past times, cafés like the Guerbois and the Nouvelle Athènes, the Opéra and the Moulin Rouge, and the Palais de l'Industrie where the first great Universal Expositions were held to show art and new techniques from all over the world. The countryside around Paris provided an inexhaustible store of subjects. The Impressionists captured the atmosphere of country towns, the Forest of Fontainebleau, and the coasts of Brittany, Normandy and Provence. They were not confined to France, however. Their art won a place in the great international markets, especially in London and New York.

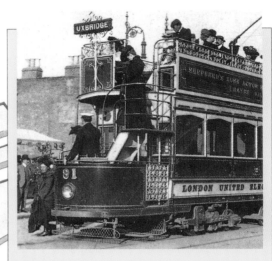

♦ LONDON

As a result of the disruption caused by the Franco-Prussian war, in 1870 the dealer Paul Durand-Ruel went to London, where he opened an art gallery in New Bond Street. Monet and Pissarro also took shelter in the English capital where they met Durand-Ruel. From then on, London became important in the story of Impressionism. Durand-Ruel arranged no fewer than eleven exhibitions at his gallery between 1870 and 1875, and three more after that. The 1905 exhibition established the movement with the English public.

Monet, *Pont de l'Europe*

ARC DE TRIOMPHE ♦

Degas, *Place de la Concorde*

Renoir, *Skaters in the Bois de Boulogne*

♦ BOIS DE BOULOGNE

S

♦ EIFFEL TOWER
(built 1889)

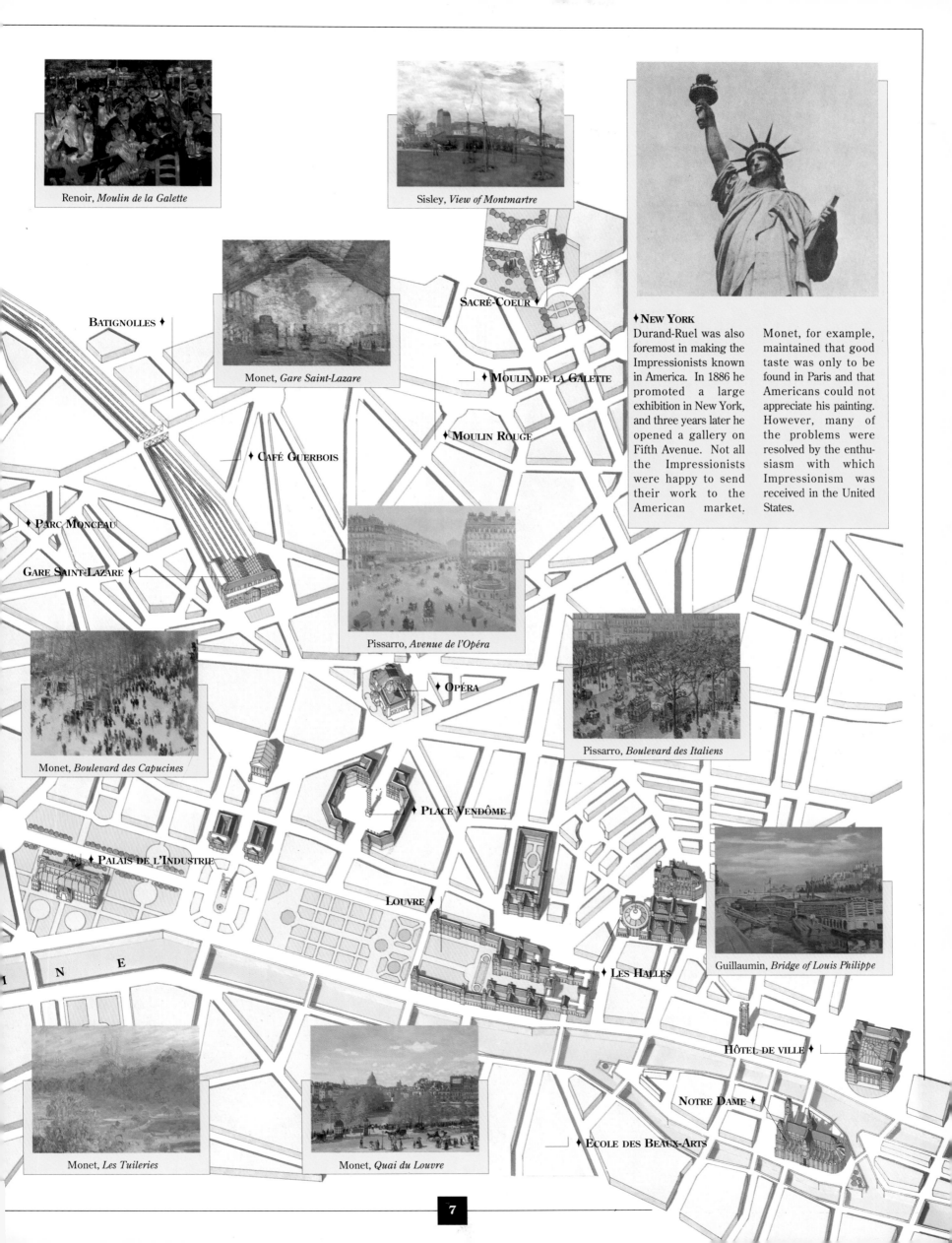

Renoir, *Moulin de la Galette*

Sisley, *View of Montmartre*

◆ SACRÉ-COEUR ◆

BATIGNOLLES ◆

Monet, *Gare Saint-Lazare*

◆ MOULIN DE LA GALETTE

◆ MOULIN ROUGE

◆ CAFÉ GUERBOIS

◆ PARC MONCEAU

GARE SAINT-LAZARE ◆

Pissarro, *Avenue de l'Opéra*

◆ OPÉRA

Pissarro, *Boulevard des Italiens*

Monet, *Boulevard des Capucines*

◆ PLACE VENDÔME

◆ PALAIS DE L'INDUSTRIE

LOUVRE ◆

Guillaumin, *Bridge of Louis Philippe*

◆ LES HALLES

S E I N E

HÔTEL DE VILLE ◆

NOTRE DAME ◆

◆ ECOLE DES BEAUX-ARTS

Monet, *Les Tuileries*

Monet, *Quai du Louvre*

◆ NEW YORK

Durand-Ruel was also foremost in making the Impressionists known in America. In 1886 he promoted a large exhibition in New York, and three years later he opened a gallery on Fifth Avenue. Not all the Impressionists were happy to send their work to the American market. Monet, for example, maintained that good taste was only to be found in Paris and that Americans could not appreciate his painting. However, many of the problems were resolved by the enthusiasm with which Impressionism was received in the United States.

THE NEW PARIS

Between 1800 and 1850 Paris grew in a chaotic fashion. The population had increased from 500,000 to one million and was concentrated in the medieval town center where social and sanitary conditions were poor. When he gained power, Napoleon III ordered a radical reorganization of the city, for which he employed Baron Haussmann, the Prefect of the Seine. In seventeen years, between 1853 and 1870, Paris changed face. Entire districts were knocked down and 20,000 houses demolished. The narrow medieval streets were replaced with avenues 40 meters (130 feet) wide - the boulevards - which criss-crossed the city and along which 40,000 modern buildings were constructed. The new Paris grew up along the boulevards. It was elegant and fashionable and loved by the Impressionists: a city of cafés, restaurants and theaters.

✦ HAUSSMANN AND NAPOLEON
Haussmann's name is synonymous with the transformation of Paris, but his work would not have been possible without the will and determination of Napoleon III. During his youth spent in England he had admired the way London was changed, and he was convinced that older districts had to be demolished in order to eliminate poverty.

✦ THE OPPONENTS
Haussmann made many enemies because of the transformation of Paris. The most famous was Victor Hugo, the great nineteenth-century French novelist and author of *Les Misérables*. The Prefect was blamed for the excessive cost of the works, the sometimes unnecessary demolition of ancient buildings, the creation of a deluxe Paris and the increased social unrest caused by the concentration of the working classes into poor and degraded suburbs.

✦ PUBLIC LAVATORIES
Another innovation: "vespasians", public urinals in the shape of kiosks.

✦ URBAN DESIGN
Haussmann did not neglect urban design. Poster columns became part of Parisian scenery.

LOOKING OUT ON THE CITY *The Man at the Window*, by Gustave Caillebotte, portrays a middle-class Parisian looking out on to one of the boulevards built during Haussmann's restructuring of the city.

REBUILDING Embankments were constructed along the banks of the Seine. The administrative buildings of the new Paris rose to replace the old houses.

NOSTALGIA In this picture the illustrator Gustave Doré expresses regret for the disappearing medieval city.

In 1853, when Haussmann began work, the future Impressionists were all very young. The oldest, Pissarro and Manet, were in their early twenties. The youngest, Cassatt and Caillebotte, were eight and five years old respectively. Their training as artists took place during the seventeen years in which Paris was transformed. They grew up with the new city. With the exception of Monet and Cassatt, they were all in Paris in 1855, when the great Universal Exposition was held at the Palais de l'Industrie. It housed the largest exhibition of painting ever seen at that time and hosted artists from twenty-eight nations. The French took the most places, especially the famous Jean Auguste Dominique Ingres and Eugène Delacroix. However, the young painters also became acquainted with work of a completely different type: in particular, canvases by an enemy of the academics, Gustave Courbet, who challenged the traditionalists, exhibiting separately in the Pavillon du Réalisme. ☞

INVISIBLE PARIS Haussmann resolved problems that had afflicted Paris for centuries. He extended the drainage system from 107 to 560 kilometers (66.5 to 348 miles). Parisians had always had little drinking water, but the new aqueducts supplied 300,000 cubic meters (10.6 million cubic feet) of water every day.

DEMOLITION La cité was the heart of the medieval city, between Notre Dame and the old Palais Royal. It was also the most ill-famed area of Paris, often described as the meeting place of thieves and murderers.

PALAIS DE L'INDUSTRIE The Palais was built in metal and glass for the Universal Exposition of 1855, the second since the London exhibition four years earlier. Later it would house the painting Salons.

COPIERS AT THE LOUVRE

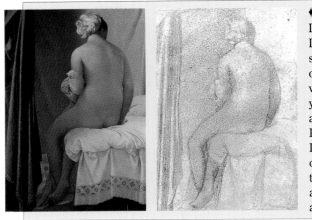

The future Impressionist painters in their youth often visited the rooms of the Louvre Museum where they were able to view masterpieces of Italian, French, Flemish and Spanish art. Here they copied the canvases of past masters. It was repetitive and tedious work, but very useful training for the painters, who could measure their ability against fine examples of great art from previous centuries. At the same time, some of them were studying at the Ecole des Beaux-Arts, which was insensitive and traditional in its teaching methods. The Ecole's aim was to train painters to produce works that would please the state and religious institutions: sacred paintings or paintings of subjects taken from mythology and ancient history.

♦ **MASTERS AND PUPILS**
At the Louvre, Renoir was attracted by eighteenth-century French masters like Watteau and Boucher. Manet preferred to copy Rembrandt and the Spanish masters. Degas made copies of Holbein, Delacroix and Ingres. Ingres was not much admired by Monet who, in fact, did not go willingly to the Louvre.

Antoine Watteau ♦ (1684-1721)

Hans Holbein ♦ (1497-1543)

Rembrandt van Rijn ♦ (1606-1668)

François Boucher ♦ (1703-1770)

☞ *The student painters who attended the Ecole des Beaux-Arts did so unwillingly. They preferred to spend their time differently. Degas, who enrolled in 1855, hardly attended at all and went on a long trip to Italy. Pissarro spent his student years in Paris in the cafés - at Fleurus, Tortoni and the Brasserie des Martyrs. He also spent time at the Académie Suisse, on the Quai des Orfèvres, which was open every day and provided with models. The old Swiss director, Julian, did not impose very strict rules on his pupils. Monet too, who came from Le Havre to Paris in 1859, attended the Académie Suisse. Before leaving for Africa, where he carried out his military service, he became friendly with Pissarro. Armand Guillaumin went to the Académie Suisse as well, and there was a touchy young man who came from Provence and was not well liked by his companions because of his abrupt manner: Paul Cézanne.* ☞

♦ Jusepe de Ribera
(1691-1652)

Eugène Delacroix ♦
(1798-1863)

♦ THE LOUVRE
The Louvre had been open to the public since the time of Napoleon I and had increased its collection of new and important works under Napoleon III.

IN THE ATELIER

In the mid-nineteenth century the studios of the most famous artists played a major role in Parisian artistic life, and were definitely more influential than the academic institutions. The atelier was not just the place where the master conceived and produced his works alone or, as was often the case, assisted by numerous helpers. The atelier was also a school. There, students learned the rudiments of life drawing, painting techniques and the master's style. What is more, the atelier was also a living-room. In the evening it was a meeting place for other painters, poets and writers, clients and art connoisseurs, friends and politicians. Pleasant hours were spent discussing subjects and ideas that were usually forbidden in official schools.

LIGHT ♦
The main requisite for an atelier was good, natural light. Large, north-facing windows were needed to provide diffused light that was not stark.

BLINDS ♦
Ample blinds were used to regulate the amount of light.

PLASTER CASTS ♦
Plaster casts, copies of famous sculptures, were typical atelier equipment. By copying the plaster casts, students began to learn about drawing.

♦ COLORS
In 1840 tubes of paint began to be produced, thus ending the custom of preparing colors in the atelier.

HEATING ♦
The furnishing of an atelier was made complete by numerous heaters, which enabled the models to remain naked for hours.

MODELS ♦
Male and female models were always present in the atelier. After an apprenticeship on plaster casts, students practiced drawing from life models. Models posed for about one hour at a time, taking fifteen-minute breaks. The master used the models for studying the poses and expressions he intended for the figures in his paintings.

POSING TABLE ♦
The table was marked so that the original position could be taken up again.

GLEYRE AND COUTURE

Charles Gleyre's *Lost Illusions* (above), painted in 1851. The young Monet was among Gleyre's students. Below, *The Romans of the Decadence*, painted by Thomas Couture in 1847, an example of the traditionalist approach to historical subjects. Couture was a famous artist, well-established in academic circles. Manet worked for six years in his studio.

After 1860, Monet, Renoir and Sisley began to frequent the studio of a Swiss painter, Charles Gleyre. It was a large, bare room with a north-facing window, a model and many young people bent over their easels. Gleyre was a generous man who did not want payment for his lessons, just contributions towards the running costs of his studio. Twice a week he corrected his students' work. He was a traditional teacher who placed much importance on drawing and insisted on the need to gain inspiration from the art of past times; but he was also fairly open to new painting methods. Manet worked in the atelier of Thomas Couture, a highly acclaimed painter, who unsuccessfully tried to make him into an academic artist. The young man painted in a new and original way while enjoying love affairs and Parisian high-society life in cafés and nightclubs. In short, he set a standard for his younger companions.

LOCATION
The most suitable locations were top floors of residential buildings. Lofts were often converted into ateliers.

PERSONAL GALLERY
The walls of the atelier were covered with paintings. In addition to the master's works, which were shown to friends and clients in a sort of personal gallery, there were also the works of friends or past painters whom the master admired.

GOOD TASTE
The atelier of a famous master was fashionably furnished.

THE MASTERS OF REALISM

Between 1850 and 1860 a new movement led by Gustave Courbet changed French painting: Realism. Reality for what it was, be it "beautiful" or "ugly", was the subject of Realist painting. The poorer classes were portrayed for the first time: workers and peasants exhausted by toil, women ironing, artisans, the poor from the cities and the countryside. Even color was used in a new way. The full and aggressive brushstrokes used by Courbet and his followers prepared the way for the technique which the Impressionists would employ when painting outdoors. The Realists caused a great scandal in academic circles. The elimination from their canvases of Greek gods and holy images seemed almost sacrilegious. In addition to Courbet, other masters were of interest to the future Impressionists: Jean François Millet, who portrayed the peasant world in his paintings, and Jean Baptiste Camille Corot, an artist who profoundly changed landscape painting.

♦ **AGAINST TRADITION**
Two paintings sent by Gustave Courbet (1819-1877) were rejected by the jury at the Paris Universal Exposition in 1855. So Courbet built the Pavillon du Réalisme, next-door, where he exhibited fifty paintings. It was the first sign of a break with tradition.

REALISTS AND ACADEMICS ♦
A cartoon by Honoré Daumier (1808-1879) on the clash between the two schools. The Realist (left) wears working-class clothes.

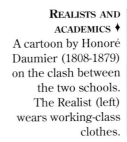

♦ **GUSTAVE COURBET**
A photograph of the master of Realism, taken around 1850.

♦ **INNOVATIONS**
Spatulas were normally used to mix colors on the palette. Realist painters also used them to spread colors on the canvas, introducing a method that would be adopted by the Impressionists.

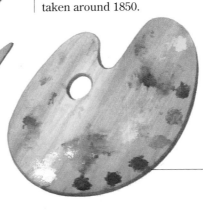

♦ **COURBET'S STUDIO**
The exact title of this painting, one of the two rejected by the Exposition in 1855, is *The painter's studio, a real allegory summing up seven years in my artistic life*. Courbet is in the middle, seated at his easel. Next to him is a child, a symbol of innocence. To the left are representatives of the working classes; on the right, writers and intellectuals, including the socialist philosopher Proudhon and the poet Baudelaire. Courbet said the painting showed "all the people who serve my cause, sustain me in my ideal and support my activity [creating art]".

♦ COROT OUTDOORS
A picture of the aged Jean Baptiste Camille Corot (1796-1875) following the Impressionist example and painting outdoors. Corot, who came into contact with Impressionist techniques late in life, believed that the finishing touches to landscapes begun outdoors should be made with accuracy in the studio.

☞ *The Brasserie des Martyrs, situated at number 9 on the rue des Martyrs, was the meeting place for members of the Realist movement. It was a smoky, noisy restaurant on three floors, with billiards, a bierkeller and private rooms. Each evening Courbet was the focus of attention in a well-fed group of intellectuals including the critic Jules Antoine Castagnary, the poet and journalist Théophile Gautier, the short-story writer Edmond Duranty, the poet Charles Baudelaire, the socialist philosopher Pierre Joseph Proudhon and many others. Manet, who belonged to a different social class, did not go. Monet and Pissarro, on the other hand, were frequent visitors in 1859 and listened from a distance to Courbet's lively arguments. They were slightly intimidated by the abrupt manner and egocentricity of this corpulent man, who was a heavy drinker and very inclined to quarrel. But they admired his method of painting and his courage when fighting his battles. Courbet did not want students, but allowed the young artists to visit his studio in rue Notre-Dame des Champs, and always gave advice and help.* ☞

♦ COROT'S LESSON
Of great importance to the Impressionists, Corot painted landscapes with open and luminous tones. *View of Ville d'Avray* is an example.

♦ COURBET AND ORNANS *The Burial at Ornans*, measuring almost 3 by 7 meters (10 by 23 feet), was exhibited at the 1851 Salon. Courbet caused a sensation by presenting a funeral in his own town as an ordinary, everyday event.

♦ MILLET'S POOR
The Gleaners, painted by Jean François Millet (1814-1875) in 1857. The portrayal of hard work in the fields, as in Millet's works, greatly influenced Courbet's Realism. It was the first time that the peasant world became fully accepted as a subject for painting. In 1848, disgusted by city life which he believed to be alienating and inhuman, Millet moved to Barbizon, a country town not far from Paris, where he spent the rest of his life.

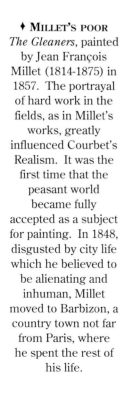

IN THE OPEN AIR

Painting "en plein air" (outdoors) was the great, unprecedented change introduced by the Impressionists. For them, painting did not mean staying behind closed doors in the cold light of a studio, but taking easel, canvas and paints and spending days in the country trying to capture the spectacle of nature, its light and colors. This was a revolutionary new idea and the painters needed new qualities. They had to work quickly because light changes so fast. They had to proceed with rapid touches of color, forgetting the idea of a preparatory drawing and putting direct on to the canvas a live impression of what they saw. Great Impressionist art was born from painting "en plein air": first the countless landscapes, then the city scenes, and the portrayal of café society and life in restaurants and public places.

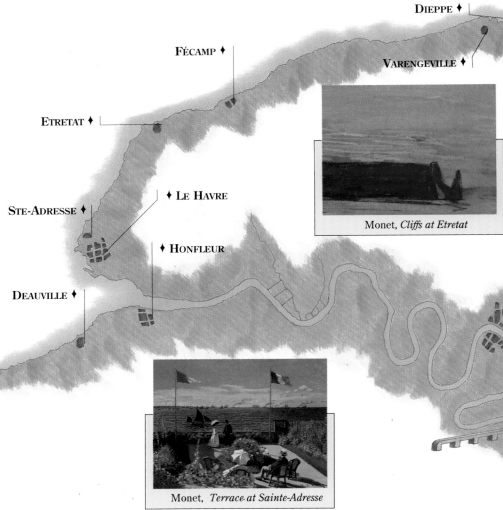

DIEPPE ♦

FÉCAMP ♦

VARENGEVILLE ♦

ETRETAT ♦

♦ LE HAVRE

STE-ADRESSE ♦

♦ HONFLEUR

DEAUVILLE ♦

Monet, *Cliffs at Etretat*

Monet, *Terrace at Sainte-Adresse*

♦ THE TRAIN
Because of the extension of rail lines, the Impressionist painters were able to travel far from Paris to reach their favorite places.

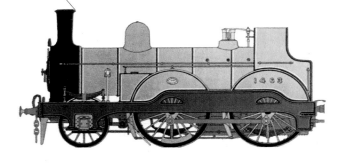

Monet, *The Artist's Garden at Giverny*

Pissarro, *Rue de l'Epicerie, Rouen*

👉 *When he returned to Paris after his military service, Monet devoted himself to painting "en plein air". In 1863, he spent the Easter holidays in Chailly, a village on the edge of the Forest of Fontainebleau, with his friend Frédéric Bazille, a painter of the same age whom he had met at Gleyre's studio. The young men spent their days in the woods and the evenings talking in the warm atmosphere of country inns like the Lion d'Or or the Cheval Blanc. At Barbizon, a town only three kilometers (1.8 miles) away, they met painters who had been devoted to landscape painting for twenty years: Théodore Rousseau, Narcisse Diaz de la Peña, Jean François Millet. Monet also went to Honfleur and Sainte-Adresse. Renoir, Bazille and Sisley chose Marlotte, a village on the edge of the Fontainebleau forest. They all developed during those years. A new painting method was born on the Normandy sea-front, on the banks of the Seine, in the forest to the south of Paris and in country towns.* 👉

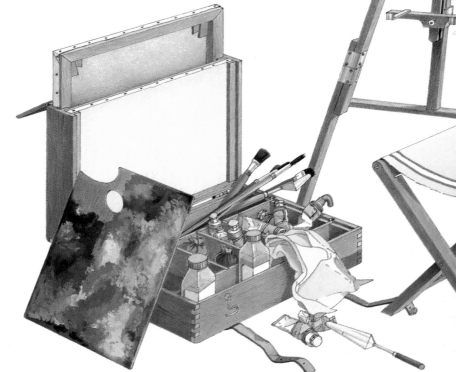

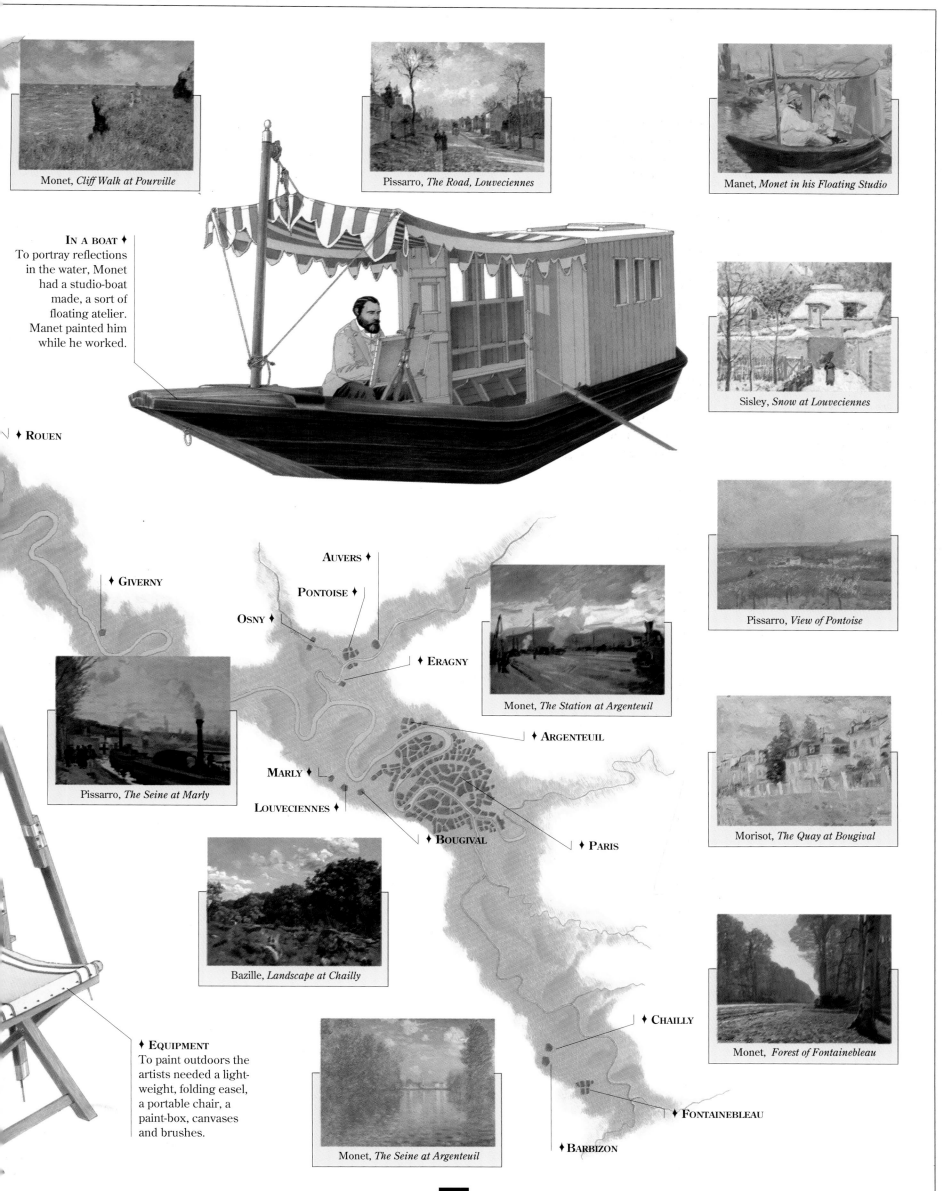

Monet, *Cliff Walk at Pourville*

Pissarro, *The Road, Louveciennes*

Manet, *Monet in his Floating Studio*

IN A BOAT ✦
To portray reflections in the water, Monet had a studio-boat made, a sort of floating atelier. Manet painted him while he worked.

Sisley, *Snow at Louveciennes*

✦ **ROUEN**

✦ **GIVERNY**

AUVERS ✦

PONTOISE ✦

OSNY ✦

✦ **ERAGNY**

Pissarro, *View of Pontoise*

Monet, *The Station at Argenteuil*

Pissarro, *The Seine at Marly*

MARLY ✦

✦ **ARGENTEUIL**

LOUVECIENNES ✦

BOUGIVAL

✦ **PARIS**

Morisot, *The Quay at Bougival*

Bazille, *Landscape at Chailly*

✦ **CHAILLY**

Monet, *Forest of Fontainebleau*

✦ EQUIPMENT
To paint outdoors the artists needed a light-weight, folding easel, a portable chair, a paint-box, canvases and brushes.

✦ **FONTAINEBLEAU**

✦ **BARBIZON**

Monet, *The Seine at Argenteuil*

NATURE

Nature is a universal theme of figurative art. However, there are many ways of approaching it and the Impressionists founded one that was completely new. In works by traditional painters, nature was often embellished or in some way changed, or was simply a background for the picture's main subject. For the Impressionists, nature spoke for itself and it was the painters' task to accept it and present it just as they saw it. Nature lives and moves, and Impressionist paintings focused much attention on all that was movement: masses of leafy branches, trees bending in the wind, reflections in the water. Also as a result of their new-found techniques, the Impressionist painters were the first to have the exceptional skill and ability needed for working fast so that they could depict spectacular moments in nature. They almost always used pure colors, without mixing them before putting them on the canvas. The paint was spread rapidly, with small, distinct brushstrokes, so that the paintings seem to be made up of luminous vibrations. The Impressionists were the first to capture on canvas what the eye sees at first glance.

♦ BEECH TREES
A forest of beeches in the fall, by the German photographer Albert Renger-Patzsch.

COUNTRYSIDE ♦
Except for Degas, the Impressionists were great landscape painters. They loved the countryside and spent a great deal of time painting "en plein air". They were interested in everything that was color and light. It was their intention to capture the spectacle of nature on canvas, exploring it in every possible way.

1. Sisley, *Wheatfields near Argenteuil*
2. Renoir, *Path Climbing Through Long Grass*

SKY ♦
Impressionist skies are in movement and varied, like their fields and seas. They are never just a background. With a few brushstrokes, the Impressionists were able to evoke a dark sky, to suggest cloud movement and oncoming rain or bright spells.

1. Renoir, *Gust of Wind*
2. Cézanne, *The Seine at Bercy*
3. Guillaumin, *The Seine at Charenton*
4. Pissarro, *February, Sunrise*

SEA ♦
The Impressionists brought a new note to seascapes, too. Water is a mobile element that changes color as it reflects light, and it is depicted in an astonishing variety of ways in the Impressionists' work. At the same time, they portrayed life at seaside holiday resorts as no-one had before.

1. Manet, *Rochefort's Escape*
2. Monet, *Terrace at Sainte-Adresse*

TREES ♦

The Impressionists often painted woods and forests, and were especially interested in all combinations of light and the shapes of tree-trunks. Monet, in particular, produced a famous series of paintings on the subject of poplars in different light conditions.

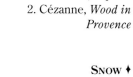

1. Monet, *Poplars*
2. Cézanne, *Wood in Provence*

SNOW ♦

Snow was also of great interest to Impressionist painters because of its ability to transform subjects and show them in a new light. Many paintings are dedicated to winter landscapes in which fields, whitened roofs, snowfalls and icy trees give nature a soft and sad atmosphere.

Monet, *The Magpie*

STILL LIFE ♦

Not all Impressionists regularly applied themselves to still life, always one of the traditional subjects of painting. More than any other, Cézanne established himself as one of the greatest masters of all time in this genre. He used still life to study the basic shapes of everyday things.

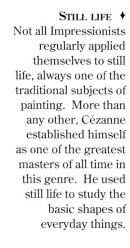

1. Cézanne, *Still Life with Apples and Biscuits*
2. Manet, *Roses and Tulips in a Dragon Vase*

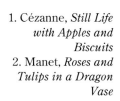

THE SALON DES REFUSÉS

The Salon was the showplace of French art. It was an exhibition held every two years at the Palais de l'Industrie. Only works chosen by a jury of academic painters were shown. For younger artists, being exhibited at the Salon was an important step in their career. If the Salon awarded them entry, they would then be able to sell their works to museums and public institutions. There was little hope of admission to the Salon for the innovators, and their chances were further diminished by the huge quantity of works submitted. In 1863 the situation became critical. Thousands of works arrived and many were rejected. Then Napoleon III went to see the rejected paintings and ordered a separate exhibition to be set up, the Salon des Refusés. Among the rejected works was one that was to become very famous, *Le Déjeuner sur l'herbe* by Manet. Public opinion and criticism were severe, but at least the rejected artists were able to exhibit their works. On the first day alone, 7,000 people visited the Salon des Refusés.

THE SALON BUILDING ✦
The Salon was held every two years. From 1855 it was housed in the Palais de l'Industrie, the metal and glass building which Napoleon III had had built for the Universal Exposition.

☞ *The Impressionists disliked academic and traditional painting, but often sent their works to the Salon jury in the hope of being accepted. Monet had no success until 1866, when he gained the admiration of the writer Emile Zola. For Manet, success alternated with rejection: in 1861 he was given an honorable mention, in 1863* Le Déjeuner sur l'herbe *was rejected. In 1865 he caused a scandal when he returned to the Salon with* Olympia. *Cézanne, disgusted by the power of the prejudiced critics, requested the establishment of a new Salon des Refusés - to no avail. The idea that the group should find a place for themselves somewhere else began to take hold.* ☞

THE ARRIVAL OF NAPOLEON ✦
When he found out about the situation at the Salon, Napoleon III decided to pay a personal visit. He saw the huge quantity of rejected works and ordered them to be shown separately at another exhibition called the Salon des Refusés.

♦ **OVERCROWDING**
This is what the store-rooms of the Palais de l'Industrie looked like before the opening of the 1863 Salon. 5,000 works had been put forward. As it was impossible to exhibit them all, 2,783 were rejected.

♦ **SHOCKING WORKS**
Le Déjeuner sur l'herbe (above) and *Olympia* were two of Manet's paintings which shocked the public and critics. The first was rejected by the 1863 Salon and shown at the Salon des Refusés. The latter, accepted by the 1865 Salon, was met with scorn like this from a critic: "Who is this odalisque with a yellow abdomen, this despicable model picked up who knows where, who poses as Olympia?"

♦ **THE ACADEMICS**
The works accepted were usually painted in the academic tradition, while the innovators' paintings were almost always rejected.

JAPANESE ART

♦ **HOKUSAI**
A self-portrait of Hokusai (above) at the age of eighty. Painter and writer Hokusai (1760-1849) was the most important Japanese artist of the last century. Active as a painter for over seventy years, he left an incredible number of prints on many different themes – landscapes, birds, female portraits – which become known first in France and then in the rest of the world. He has greatly influenced painting and, more recently, advertising, comic strips and cartoon films. The Impressionists were fascinated by his art, which they studied in depth and from which they gained much inspiration.

The second Universal Exposition, held in Paris in 1867, was of particular importance. This was not so much because of the thousands of handicrafts and industrial products on show - ranging from Krupp cannons to American rocking-chairs - but more because of the presence of a Japanese section. It was the first time that the general public could view a large display of art and crafts from that distant and almost unknown country. Although the Impressionists had already seen some rare examples of Japanese art that were in circulation in Paris at that time, they were very excited. Their work was reinforced and stimulated by the Japanese painting which they were now able to study further. They admired its freedom of composition and perspective, the use of pure, clean colors and the elimination of superfluous detail.

♦ **A FAN**
This printed fan, the work of Kuniyoshi, a Japanese artist, is an example of the objects which attracted the Impressionists' attention.

♦ **A STRANGE EPISODE**
Knowledge of Hokusai's art in France dated back to a strange episode. In 1856, as the painter Félix Braquemond was unwrapping some porcelain that had come from Japan, he realized to his amazement that the wrapping paper was in fact pages from a book of Hokusai prints. He hurried to show them to his artist friends.

♦ MARY CASSATT AND JAPAN The two pictures on the left, watercolors by Mary Cassatt, *The Hairstyle* and *Woman Bathing*, show how the artist was inspired by Japanese prints.

MONET AND JAPAN ♦ In 1876 Monet painted his wife Camille wearing a kimono, in a work entitled *The Japanese Woman.*

♦ THE WATERLILY BRIDGE Monet moved to the country town of Giverny on the Seine, in 1883, and built a bridge of oriental design over his pond there. It was inspired by bridges like the one in the Japanese print on the right. On the left, *The Japanese Bridge in Giverny,* one of Monet's many paintings of his "waterlily bridge".

☞ *With the exception of Cézanne and Renoir, who were indifferent to what they considered a passing fashion, the Impressionists were fascinated by Japanese art. They were frequent visitors and clients of a shop called "The Chinese Door" in the rue de Rivoli, where prints, porcelain, fans, costumes and various Japanese handicrafts were displayed. Degas collected a very large number of prints. In 1876 Monet portrayed his wife dressed in a kimono and surrounded by fans. Later, in his garden at Giverny, he had a Japanese bridge built, a copy of the bridges he had seen in Hokusai's works. However, Mary Cassatt was the artist most influenced by Japanese painting.* ☞

PHOTOGRAPHY

Photography became available to people towards the middle of the nineteenth century and invaded an area that had always been the preserve of painting. Photographers as well as painters could now produce portraits, scenes and illustrations. Many artists regarded the novelty with suspicion and concern. The poet Baudelaire called it a banal imitation of real art. The Impressionists, however, felt that photography was a powerful way to study reality and therefore a very useful aid in their research. Photography permitted them to analyze movement, to notice details that would normally escape the eye, to study subjects carefully, to capture fleeting moments and to collect "impressions" and store them for working on later. They became friendly with the photographer Nadar, who would later house their first exhibition.

♦ **FROM CAMERA OBSCURA TO PHOTOGRAPHY**
Artists used the camera obscura to help them draw perspectives. Now attempts were made to fix the images produced on the camera obscura's screen. In France in 1829 the lithographer Niepce and the painter Daguerre agreed to combine the results of their experiments with light-sensitive chemicals. However, it was the younger Daguerre alone who in 1839 announced the process he had perfected: a silver-plated sheet sensitized with iodine vapor was exposed in a camera for up to half an hour, until a scarcely visible image appeared on it; this image was then developed by treating the plate with mercury vapor, and fixed by washing it in salt solution.

THE PLATE ♦
The light-sensitive plate was contained in a covered plate-holder. Having framed and focused the image on the ground-glass screen, the photographer inserted the plate in place of the screen, removed the cover, and let in light through the lens.

THE LENS ♦
In a movable tube the lens was used to make the image sharp.

EXPOSURE ♦
The lens cover was removed and replaced to control the length of the exposure.

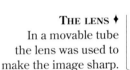

THE COLOR WHEEL ♦
Chevreul designed this wheel to show relationships between colors. Those on the blue side are called "cold colors" and seem to move backwards. Those on the red side, called "hot colors", seem to move forwards.

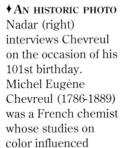

♦ **AN HISTORIC PHOTO**
Nadar (right) interviews Chevreul on the occasion of his 101st birthday. Michel Eugène Chevreul (1786-1889) was a French chemist whose studies on color influenced the Impressionists' painting technique.

NADAR IN A BALLOON ♦
Félix Nadar, the greatest French photographer, was the first to use a hot-air balloon for aerial photography. This was the precursor of modern aerial photography.

♦ MOVEMENT
Eadweard James Muybridge (1830-1904) created a camera to photograph moving figures. His book *Animal Locomotion*, written in 1875, was a great success among artists.

DEGAS AND PHOTOGRAPHY ♦
After the Bath - Woman Drying Herself. Degas took the photograph and painted from it, in 1896.

♦ GLASS SCREEN
The photographer used the ground-glass screen at the back of the camera to frame and focus the image.

♦ BELLOWS
The photographer used the bellows to adjust the focus.

AN EARLY SNAPSHOT ♦
A photo by Pierre Petit shows building work on the Statue of Liberty, which was constructed between 1876 and 1881.

FROM ON HIGH ♦
Place de l'Etoile, photographed by Nadar from a hot-air balloon.

Paris was the most important center of study for photographic art. This was due mainly to pioneers like Félix Nadar, who produced numerous portraits and city scenes during the Haussmann years. The Impressionists' encounter with photography was a further stimulus to their work. They often painted people in a new perspective, and they stepped up their outdoor painting activities in the country, despite serious financial difficulties. Sometimes they did not even have enough money to buy food. In 1869, Monet, who had many of his paintings requisitioned by his creditors, asked Bazille for help: "Dear Friend, Do you want to know the situation I find myself in? Ask Renoir who brings us bread from his house so that we don't die. We have been without bread, cooking fuel and light for eight days...."

PEOPLE

The sense of spontaneity achieved in Impressionist portraits would have been inconceivable without photography. Photography provided the painters with new images of their subjects and the places where they lived. Impressionist portraits differed from traditional ones because of the attention they gave to the surroundings in which the person was placed rather than because they were sensitive or exact likenesses. The subjects were no longer isolated, abstract figures with the cold appearance of someone posing. They lived in the paintings, together with the objects, scenery and light surrounding them. Although given special characteristics, they were almost an object among many others and seemed absorbed into their setting. The human body was no longer treated as an abstract, anatomical model. Modern men and women were seen in their everyday behavior: the way they dressed, their social life, at home, in the street. They could be playing the piano, working in the office, waiting in the wings to go on stage, or even leaning on a gaming-table. The pose was never without meaning, even if the figure was resting, as this moment was just as much a part of someone's life as the more active ones.

✦ **FIRST SNAPSHOTS**
A portrait photographer at work, photographed in 1886 by Alfred Stieglitz.

CHILDREN ✦
The Impressionists often painted portraits of children. The world of childhood appealed to them because it offered a wide variety of themes, and subjects who were unused to posing.

1. Degas, *The Bellelli Family*
2. Manet, *The Fifer*
3. Degas, *Hortense Valpinçon*
4. Manet, *Boy Blowing Soap Bubbles*
5. Renoir, *The Children's Afternoon at Wargemont*

THE BOURGEOISIE ✦
The middle classes were the subject of an infinite number of Impressionist paintings. Scenes chosen were of ordinary, everyday life. People were portrayed at work, during their free time, or enjoying their favorite pastimes.

1. Degas, *The Cotton Exchange, New Orleans*
2. Degas, *At the Stock Exchange*
3. Manet, *The Balcony*
4. Cassatt, *Lady at the Tea Table*
5. Renoir, *M and Mme Bernheim de Villers*

THE POOR ✦
The poor were also a new object of the painters' attention. Those who carried out the menial tasks required by modern city life - the waiters, ironing women and floorscrapers - became the subjects of Impressionist paintings.

1. Manet, *The Beer Waitress*
2. Pissarro, *The Pork Butcher*
3. Renoir, *Young Woman Sewing*
4. Degas, *A Woman Ironing*
5. Caillebotte, *The Floorscrapers*

The Impressionists as seen by the Impressionists: as well as developing the tradition of self-portraiture, they liked to paint each other. They saw each other often, as friends. Manet painted Berthe Morisot with whom he had a deep and sincere friendship. Monet and Renoir often worked "en plein air" together and on the same subjects, so spent a great deal of time in each other's company. The originality of Impressionist portraits lies in the absence of interest in reflecting the subject's mood and in the ability to break down the composition into pure, visual values. For the Impressionists, a face was an object like any other, made up of color, light and shade.

1. Degas, *Self-Portrait*
2. Cézanne, *Self-Portrait*
3. Manet, *Berthe Morisot in a Black Hat, with a Bunch of Violets*
4. Caillebotte, *Self-Portrait*
5. Renoir, *Claude Monet Reading*

THE NUDE ♦

The Impressionists left tradition behind when painting nudes. Their paintings were never cold like the products of the ateliers. They did not always use professional models and the poses have a freshness and spontaneity of their own.

1. Cézanne, *The Large Bathers*
2. Degas, *The Tub*
3. Renoir, *Nude in the Sunlight*
4. Renoir, *Nana*

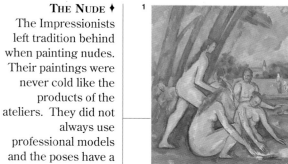

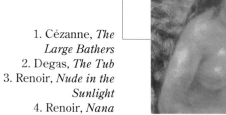

LA GRENOUILLÈRE

On a minor arm of the Seine, between Chatou and Bougival, was La Grenouillère, a floating café flanked by swimming baths used by Parisians for Sunday outings and entertainment. Boat-races were organized at La Grenouillère, where people also swam, ate in the small restaurant and danced in the evening. For some time, Monet and Renoir had been comparing their work on the same subjects, and in 1869 they both portrayed La Grenouillère on canvases of almost the same size, painted "en plein air" from the same observation point. In capturing with such immediacy the gentle, fashionable atmosphere, these two paintings define the Impressionist style, and could be considered among the first complete examples of Impressionism.

✦ THE POSTER
A poster advertised the entertainment Parisians would find at La Grenouillère, which was easily reached by the first railway built in France, between Paris and Saint-Germain.

THE FROG POOL ✦
"La Grenouillère" means "frog pool". The central island, dominated by a large tree, also had a name: "camembert", because it was shaped like the cheese.

THE ISLAND ✦
This was the focal point of the establishment.

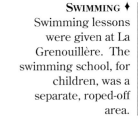

SWIMMING ✦
Swimming lessons were given at La Grenouillère. The swimming school, for children, was a separate, roped-off area.

THE VISITORS ✦
People in bathing suits and elegantly dressed customers.

✦ BAZILLE'S BATHERS
Bathing in the Seine was a popular pastime of Parisians during the summer. Bazille, who painted this canvas in 1869, was among several painters interested in the subject of bathers.

☛ *While Monet and Renoir, who shared a studio for a while, were busy at La Grenouillère, the other Impressionists were also developing rapidly. Pissarro was working in Pontoise and Louveciennes, where his painting became clearer and lighter. Manet travelled a great deal. He visited Spain and England and would sometimes adopt the "en plein air" method. Cézanne also began to work outdoors. Degas became interested in the theater world, which he was to portray often. But times were hard, and not only because of the many rejections from the Salon. Monet, who had a son by his model Camille Doncieux in 1867, was still in serious financial difficulty. He was sometimes unable to paint because he could not afford to buy materials. Pissarro, whose father died in 1865, was also very short of money. Cézanne isolated himself more and more in Aix-en-Provence. For Sisley, who had recently married and had a child, these were the last tranquil years before the death of his father, ruined by the war, left him in dire financial straits.* ☛

♦ **SAILING**
This was one of La Grenouillère's sporting attractions. It appears that Bazille, Monet and Renoir took part in the Bougival boat-races.

♦ **BOAT RENTAL**
Beneath the restaurant there were wooden rowing boats to be hired for short trips on the Seine.

MONET'S COMPOSITION ♦
Everything becomes a matter of light in Monet's composition, and detail is reduced to a minimum. Monet makes more space for the water, which is the real subject of his painting.

♦ **RENOIR'S STUDIES**
Renoir paid more attention to the leaves on the trees and to people's clothing. He differentiated between the colors of the boats and, albeit sketchily, drew some of the figures in the background.

BATIGNOLLES

Never before had a city district and a café been the center of an important artistic movement. The first time this happened was with the Impressionists in Paris. The district was the Batignolles quarter, near Montmartre, where many painters set up their studios. The café was the Guerbois, at 11 rue des Batignolles, now avenue de Clichy. Just as they moved their workplace out of doors, into the countryside and the new urban developments, so the Impressionists moved their discussions outside the atelier. Cafés offered Parisians both refreshment and entertainment. There were many kinds: those frequented by intellectuals and artists, those frequented by politicians and financiers and those for the working class. They were bustling and pleasant places. At the Guerbois the Impressionists exchanged opinions in a free and lively way.

♦ LA "TERRASSE"
Cafés could now extend onto the pavements of the broad boulevards. Their awnings became an unmistakable feature of Paris.

♦ DEGAS
Small and slender, Degas made brief appearances at the café. Of exceptional intelligence, he was greatly feared for his sharp tongue.

♦ RENOIR
Although poor and modest, he was always cheerful and funny. Everyone at the Guerbois enjoyed his friendliness and geniality that defused even the most heated discussion.

♦ BAZILLE
Blond, tall, slender and distinguished-looking. Although Bazille was a little shy, he was one of the very few capable of countering the arguments of Manet and Degas.

♦ MANET
Of medium height, blond, mocking and witty, Manet was the focus of attention in the group and dominated discussions.

♦ ZOLA
Short, chubby and very energetic, the writer was coming very close to success during the Guerbois days. He spoke calmly and forcefully, always siding with the innovative artists.

LA TAVERNE POUSSET
An elegant, high-society Parisian café and typical meeting place for intellectuals, politicians and "bons viveurs".

THE CAFÉ
In a sketch of 1869, seemingly inspired by the Café Guerbois, Manet creates the atmosphere of an artists' meeting place. Manet and all those concerned with the future of the new movement gathered around a few marble-topped tables at the café.

MONET
Monet used to sit by himself, partly because he felt less well-versed than the others and partly because he thought the discussions of little use. Nonetheless the café was an antidote to long periods of isolation in the country.

PISSARRO
He lived at Louveciennes, but whenever in Paris he visited the Guerbois where he was always a welcome guest. He was the only one with a clear political philosophy, a socialist with anarchist tendencies.

THE STUDIO
In 1870 Henri Fantin-Latour, a painter and friend of Manet and frequent visitor to the Guerbois, portrayed a studio in the Batignolles quarter. Manet, in the middle, is painting a portrait of Astruc. Renoir, Bazille and Monet can be recognized among the artists standing.

CÉZANNE
Tall, thin and slightly round-shouldered, he sat in a corner and listened. He did not go to the Guerbois often. He was fairly unsociable and would sometimes leave if he did not agree with what was being said.

ASTRUC
Poet and sculptor and defender of the new painting method, Zacharie Astruc was very close to Manet.

☞ *It was Manet, in 1868, who discovered the Café Guerbois in a district that had been on the outskirts at one time and had kept its provincial air. Manet, Monet, Degas, Cézanne, Zola, Sisley, Pissarro and Bazille all met at the Guerbois, which was not very elegant but had a billiard hall, a garden and a pergola for wedding receptions. They discussed the best way to exhibit their works now that they had broken away from academic art. Manet was the main figure. He was witty and intelligent and able to destroy an adversary with one quip. Degas was also feared for his sharp tongue, although he maintained his lordly, aristocratic manner and did not seem to feel completely at ease in the unruly atmosphere of the Guerbois. The atmosphere could be somewhat too lively: according to an article in "Paris Journal", Manet challenged the writer and critic Edmond Duranty to a duel and slightly wounded him.* ☞

Meeting Places

Cafés, restaurants, open-air meeting places, dance halls: fashionable Parisian life was no longer just for the nobility but for the emerging middle class whose values were very different. Life had both a light and a dark side. On the one hand there were frivolous love affairs, the pleasures of eating well, nightclubs and entertainment. On the other hand there were negative aspects like prostitution and alcoholism. In their paintings the Impressionists worked tirelessly on the theme of cafés and meeting places. It was here that they found real Parisian life and the new rising classes which, along with city scenes, were their favorite subjects. As always, their portrayals were not meant as either adverse or favorable social comment. All the characters involved in Parisian social life are to be found in their paintings: the waitress at the Folies-Bergère bar and the woman drinking absinthe, the members of the orchestra and the audience attending performances at the Opéra, the bourgeoisie listening to concerts in the Tuileries, the musicians playing in open-air cafés, and the prostitutes who worked in the restaurants and hotels.

♦ **THE MOULIN ROUGE** In this lithograph of 1891 Henri de Toulouse-Lautrec depicts the nightclub and its main attraction, "La Goulue", a dancer who performed there every night.

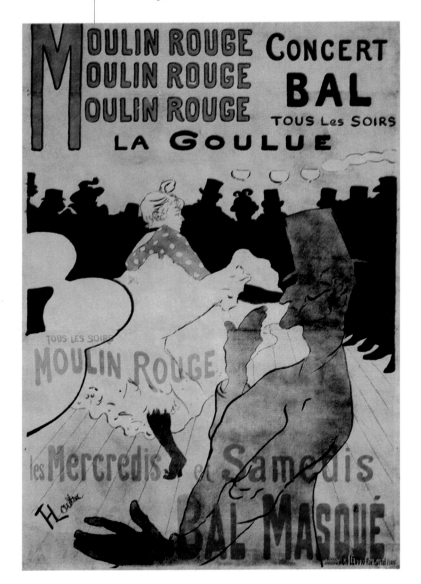

THE CAFÉ AND RESTAURANT ♦ Cafés and restaurants played a key role in the life of Paris and small French cities. Neither the nobility nor the countryfolk of the old society frequented restaurants. It was only with the emergence of the middle class that eating out began to be considered as entertainment rather than a necessity. It was an opportunity to meet and spend time with family and friends.

1. Renoir, *The Boating Party*
2. Manet, *Chez Père Lathuille*
3. Degas, *Women on a Café Terrace*
4. Manet, *A Bar at the Folies-Bergère*
5. Renoir, *At the Inn of Mother Anthony*

THE RACETRACK ♦ On public holidays Parisians enjoyed watching horse-racing. The racecourse was a fashionable place to meet, and they were excited by the lively, competitive atmosphere, the speed of the races, and the close relationship between animal and man. Many Impressionist painters, especially Manet and Degas, liked to paint scenes from race meetings at the Longchamps course.

1. Degas, *Racehorses in front of the Stands*
2. Manet, *Horse-Racing at Longchamps*
3. Degas, *The Gentlemen's Race: Before the Start*
4. Degas, *At the Races*

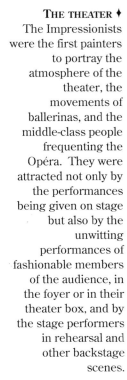

THE THEATER ♦

The Impressionists were the first painters to portray the atmosphere of the theater, the movements of ballerinas, and the middle-class people frequenting the Opéra. They were attracted not only by the performances being given on stage but also by the unwitting performances of fashionable members of the audience, in the foyer or in their theater box, and by the stage performers in rehearsal and other backstage scenes.

1. Manet, *Masked Ball at the Opéra*
2. Degas, *Café-concert*
3. Degas, *The Star*

DANCING ♦

In cities and in the country, in Parisian suburbs and small provincial towns, the nineteenth-century French were infected by a new fever: dancing. It rose above the barriers of class distinction to affect everyone, rich and poor alike. Many Impressionist paintings recreate the atmosphere of dance halls in different parts of France. And the painters also used dances as a setting for pictures on related themes such as courting and meeting.

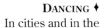

1. Renoir, *Le Moulin de la Galette*
2. Renoir, *A Dance in the Country*
3. Renoir, *A Dance in the City*

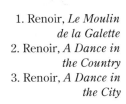

WAR AND THE COMMUNE

♦ NADAR'S HOT-AIR BALLOON
The photographer Nadar took part in the defense of Paris by organizing flights behind enemy lines in hot-air balloons from which he called for resistance.

Great and dramatic events took place in 1870 and 1871: war between France and Prussia and the French defeat, followed by revolt in Paris where the citizens rose up and established a revolutionary republic called "La Commune". Paris was beset by civil war. The Impressionist painters continued their work during these exceptional events. In a series of sketches and lithographs, Manet described starkly the devastation of the city. But finally, with Paris in chaos, it seemed that not even art could be revived. A friend of Pissarro wrote: "Paris is empty and will become even emptier. You would think that there had never been any painters and artists in Paris."

♦ THE VENDÔME COLUMN Courbet ordered the sailors of the Commune to knock down the Vendôme column, a symbol of Napoleonic power. After the Commune was crushed in May 1871, he was ordered to pay for its reconstruction. In desperation, he took refuge in Switzerland.

♦ COURBET AND THE INSURGENTS
Gustave Courbet photographed with the sailors who destroyed the Vendôme column.

♦ **BAZILLE'S DEATH**
The only one of the Impressionists to fight, Frédéric Bazille, here in a portrait by Renoir, enrolled in the Zouaves regiment (the French light infantry). He was killed on November 28, 1870, during the battle of Beaune-le-Roland.

THE BARRICADES ♦
Manet stayed in Paris during the Prussian siege, but was not there during the Commune.

The Barricade, right, is one of a series of lithographs dedicated to these tragic episodes of French history.

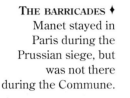

☛ *War ended life at the Guerbois. France's defeat at Sedan on September 2, 1870 brought about the fall of Napoleon III. The war continued and Paris surrendered to the Prussians in January 1871. The painters took various action: Manet enrolled in the National Guard, Degas in the artillery, Renoir in the cavalry. Bazille was killed in November 1870 before reaching his thirtieth birthday. The others evacuated to avoid the war: Monet and Pissarro went to London, Cézanne to Aix-en-Provence. Monet and Pissarro worked together in the English capital. "We were full of enthusiasm for the London scenes," says Pissarro. "Monet worked in the parks, I studied the effects of fog, snow and the spring." Meanwhile in Paris, the master of Realism, Courbet, a man with radical beliefs, was appointed Head of Fine Arts by the Commune. After the bloody repression of the Commune, he was arrested.* ☛

♦ **DEATH AND DEVASTATION**
The result of the war and the repression of the Commune: 17,000 dead, Paris in chaos, l'Hôtel de Ville, the Tuileries, and the Palais Royal, together with hundreds of houses and shops, burned down. Thousands of Communards were sentenced to death and deportation.

THE 1874 EXHIBITION

On April 15, 1874, at 35 boulevard des Capucines, in the studio belonging to the photographer Nadar, the group's first, historic exhibition was held, showing the best of the Impressionist painters' work after a period of exceptional creativity. The exhibition was promoted by the Société anonyme des artistes, peintres, sculpteurs, graveurs, founded by thirty artists one year earlier. The object of the association was to give its members the chance to exhibit and sell their works without invitation or acceptance by a jury. Degas, Pissarro, Renoir, Monet, Sisley, Morisot, Guillaumin and Cézanne took part in the exhibition. Manet was absent. A total of 163 works were shown. The date was carefully chosen: the Salon was to open two weeks later and the Société wanted to avoid giving the impression that it was an exhibition of rejected works. However, the reaction of the public and the critics was negative and the exhibition ended in failure.

♦ A NEW JOURNAL
An issue of "L'Impressioniste", the magazine of the Société anonyme des artistes, peintres, sculpteurs, graveurs, founded by Monet and his friends in 1873. After their first exhibition in 1874, the Société organized a further seven: in 1876, 1877, 1879, 1880, 1881, 1882 and 1886.

♦ THE CATALOGUE
The title-page of the catalogue of the first exhibition held by the Impressionist painters. Edmond Renoir, brother of Pierre Auguste, produced the catalogue.

♦ SATIRE
In a satirical cartoon, Impressionist paintings were used to frighten enemy soldiers.

♦ THE FIRST IMPRESSION
This may not be Monet's finest painting, but it is certainly the painting which symbolizes the birth of the group. It is titled *Impression: Sunrise*, and was the work, scorned by critics, that gave rise to the term "Impressionism".

♦ AN HISTORIC PLACE
The studio of the photographer Nadar, in the boulevard des Capucines, where the exhibition of April 1874 was held.

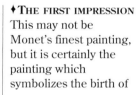

CÉZANNE ♦
He showed three works at the 1874 exhibition. *The House of the Hanged Man*, painted in 1873-74, is one of his most famous early works.

PISSARRO ♦
He exhibited five paintings including this image of a winter sunrise in the countryside, *Hoarfrost*, painted in 1873.

DEGAS ♦
He exhibited ten works. *Carriage at the Races*, painted between 1870 and 1872, is an example of the interest in horse-racing, which also attracted Manet.

☞ *A new regime, the Third Republic, was established in France after the defeat at Sedan. All the painters returned to Paris and began work again. Their meeting place was again a café, the Nouvelle Athènes, on the corner of the Place Pigalle. The years following 1870 were also years of intense work "en plein air". Together with Manet and Renoir, Monet worked in Argenteuil. Pissarro took up residence in Louveciennes and Cézanne and Guillaumin in Pontoise. By 1874, only a few critics had understood the changes made by the Impressionists and reacted positively. The organization of the exhibition was unsuccessful. It was seen by 3,500 visitors, but few paintings were sold and for low prices. Some of the artists, like Degas and Morisot, did not sell at all. The number of unsold works was so great that another exhibition was organized the following year at the Hôtel Drouot, at which Monet's works were valued at between 150 and 300 francs and some of Renoir's at under 100 francs. These were very low sums, considering that a bricklayer's weekly wage was about 50 francs.* ☞

MORISOT ♦
She exhibited nine works including *The Cradle*, painted in 1873, which shows her interest in indoor and family scenes. Morisot continued to work on these subjects throughout her painting career.

MONET ♦
Of the twelve works exhibited by Monet, *Boulevard des Capucines, Paris*, painted in 1873, was considered one of the most "scandalous" because of the sketchy way in which the city promenaders are painted.

RENOIR ♦
He exhibited seven works. *The Box at the Opéra*, painted in 1874, is one of the first Impressionist works dedicated to the theater. Renoir took an active part in setting up the exhibition, having the difficult task of bringing together works that were very different from each other.

THE CITY

The Impressionists were the first painters to depict the modern city, and Paris, rebuilt by Haussmann, was the most modern city in Europe. They were not interested only in showing its characteristic corners but also portrayed the new spacious atmosphere of the wide boulevards and open areas and scenes of city life. Viewing the banks of the Seine, the parks, the stations, the Impressionists saw the city as something mobile and alive, with its busy bourgeoisie, workers, gentlemen and ladies promenading or resting. They paid special attention to public events. The images of Paris seen in the paintings of Monet or Manet, Renoir or Caillebotte tell us more about life in an industrial city than a history book. While traditional painters produced only broad city views, the Impressionists explored every aspect, including the outermost suburbs and poorest districts, which became one of the most important subjects of their artistic studies.

♦ **PARISIAN HOUSING**
Section through a Parisian apartment building of the kind constructed along the boulevards during Haussmann's redevelopment of the city. The wealthier classes lived on the first floor. The higher the floor, the lower the social class: the middle classes would live on the second floor, white-collar workers on the third. The poorer people, servants, students and artists, lived in the garrets on the top floor.

PANORAMAS ♦
In order to show the spaciousness of the city, the Impressionists painted many scenes viewed from above. From these we can appreciate the broad, new spaces opened up during the rebuilding of Paris. Other attractive subjects were bridges, which were essential thoroughfares in a city where people moved around much more than before.

1. Monet, *Jardin de l'Infante*
2. Pissarro, *Boieldieu Bridge, Rouen*
3. Renoir, *Pont Neuf*

CROWDS ♦
Unlike the narrow streets of the medieval city center, the wide boulevards were always crowded with people. The Impressionists depicted the crowds, and were the first to paint a city that was lively even after dark.

1. Monet, *Boulevard des Capucines*
2. Monet, *Rue Montorgueil Decked out with Flags*
3. Pissarro, *Boulevard Montmartre*

PROMENADES IN THE CITY ♦
The middle class promenading is another subject that was dear to the Impressionists. There are paintings of men and women, family groups and lone figures against a background of the new city squares and broad, airy boulevards designed by Haussmann.

1. Monet, *Quai du Louvre*
2. Caillebotte, *Paris, A Rainy Day*
3. Renoir, *Place Clichy*

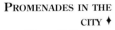

THE ART MARKET

The Impressionists not only revolutionized art but also were involved in revolutionizing the art market. Until the second half of the nineteenth century, the academic authorities, who wanted religious or historical subjects, used the Salon to control painters' activities and fixed the prices of works that were then acquired by public institutions and a few wealthy buyers. With the Impressionists, a new individual appeared on the scene: the art dealer, who collected works, even those of young artists who were not yet established, and sold them on the private market. The art dealer was a self-financing entrepreneur. Therefore, it was in his own interests to promote his artists' work, even in the most distant countries. Impressionist paintings now reached the English and American markets and ended up in collections and museums throughout the world.

MANET ♦
The Balcony, 1869, sold at the Manet studio auction in 1884. Bought by Caillebotte for 3,000 francs.

MONET ♦
Camille (The Green Dress), 1886, sold to Arsène Houssaye, Fine Arts inspector and editor of "L'Artiste", for 800 francs in 1868.

RENOIR ♦
Pont Neuf, 1872, sold for 300 francs at the auction of unsold works at the Hôtel Drouot on March 24, 1875.

MONET ♦
Blue House in Zaandam, 1871-72, part of the Hoschedé collection sold at auction in 1874 for 405 francs.

SISLEY ♦
Floods at Port-Marly, 1876, sold at the Faure collection auction in 1878 for 180 francs. After Sisley died in 1900, the painting was sold for 43,000 francs, more than Sisley had earned in his whole life.

♦ THE AUCTION ROOM
All the Paris auctions were held at the Hôtel Drouot, under governmental supervision. In 1875 the sale of Impressionist paintings that had not been purchased at the group's first exhibition the year before was held here.

♦ **PAUL DURAND-
RUEL**
1831-1922
He was the first
dealer to invest in the
Impressionists.

♦ **VICTOR CHOQUET**
1821-1891
He bought
Impressionist
paintings, especially
Cézanne, but also
admired past
masters.

♦ **GEORGES PETIT**
1856-1920
He crossed Durand-
Ruel, taking control
of many of the artists
and organizing
important exhibitions
in his own gallery,
which can be seen in
this print.

☛ *Financed and organized by Gustave Caillebotte, the Impressionist group's second exhibition was held in 1876 at Paul Durand-Ruel's gallery in rue Le Peletier. Yet again the reaction of critics was, for the most part, hostile. These were fertile years, however, especially for Monet and Renoir. Then the group began to disband. Each member started to follow his own personal path and even friendships were no longer close. Cézanne isolated himself in Aix-en-Provence, Pissarro went to Pontoise, Sisley to Marly-le-Roi. Success was now finally gained. In 1881 Manet was awarded the Legion of Honor. Monet and Renoir were admitted to the Salon. Paul Durand-Ruel, an art dealer who had met Monet in London and who was to play a key role in the Impressionists' success, worked hard to promote their painting. It was through him that they gained international fame.* ☛

♦ **CÉZANNE**
The House of the Hanged Man, 1873-74, purchased by Camondo at the Choquet sale of 1899 for 6,200 francs.

♦ **RENOIR**
Pont des Arts, Paris, 1867, sold for 70 francs at the auction of unsold works at the Hôtel Drouot on March 24, 1875.

The portal, morning fog

The portal, morning effect

The portal, harmony in blue

The portal, harmony in brown

LIGHT

The Impressionists revolutionized the way nature was seen and depicted. They chose new subjects to paint and portrayed city life for the first time. Above all, however, they saw everything in a new light. For an Impressionist, light could be the true subject of a canvas, and a figure, building or landscape simply a pretext for exploring the various conditions of light. The most important example is Monet who, between 1892 and 1894, produced fifty different paintings of Rouen Cathedral seen in all possible conditions: in sun and rain, at dawn and sunset, in summer and winter. Monet was not

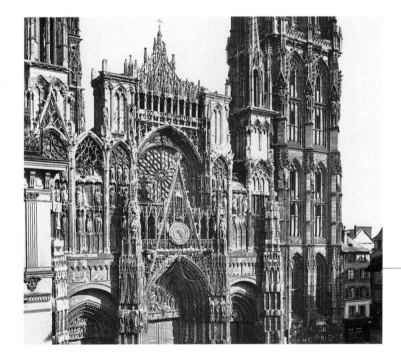

♦ THE SUBJECT
Built in the thirteenth century, Rouen Cathedral is one of the most important monuments of French Gothic architecture. In order to paint his series of façades, Monet set himself up on the second floor of a shop opposite, but later decided to finish his work in the studio without being able to view the monument.

Harmony in blue and gold, bright sun   *The portal, sunshine*   *Rouen Cathedral, sun effect, late in the day*   *Symphony in grey and pink*

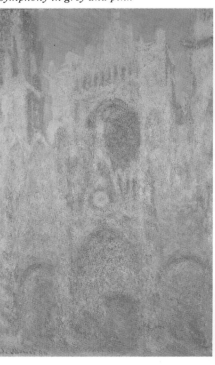

The portal, harmony in grey, dull weather   *Rouen Cathedral, the portal*   *Rouen Cathedral, the portal*   *The portal, midday*

concerned with showing the structure of the cathedral, but with observing how its structure seemed to change before his eyes as the light changed. He does not even show the whole monument, but only part of it. The Rouen cycle is one of the masterpieces of Impressionist painting, and the greatest example of theme painting, a series on the same subject. Monet's Waterlily canvases are another example. Producing fifty canvases on the same subject was completely new in painting history. By working continually on one subject, Monet displayed his idea of the painter's mission: since there is not just one view of reality, the painter should not fix his subject but be able to portray it as it is constantly changing.

♦ THE SEASONS
The four images on the left are computer simulations of light conditions at Rouen Cathedral just as Monet would have seen it during different seasons and at different times of the day. Clockwise, from top left, the light conditions at 2 p.m. on December 23, at 2 p.m. on March 21, at 2 p.m. and at 7 p.m. on June 21.

The portal and Alban Tower, dull weather   *Harmony in white*   *The portal, sunshine*   *The portal and Alban Tower, dawn*

THEIR LEGACY

At the end of the Impressionist period, there was an understanding of how the painters had changed the whole art scene. When Manet and the other members of the group began their work, art was still firmly in the hands of the academic institutions. When they finished, all artists were free to follow their own instinct and own individual talent. The old rules for learning drawing and applying color no longer held sway. Nor were there any exclusive rules governing what could or could not be painted: contemporary life was fully acknowledged as a subject for art. Through decades of study that revolutionized the method and very concept of painting, the Impressionists had smoothed the way for painters following after them. Impressionism is at the root of all modern art, because it was the first movement that managed to free itself from preconceived ideas, and because it changed not only the way life was depicted but the way life was seen.

♦ EUGÈNE DELACROIX
1798-1863

♦ PABLO PICASSO
1881-1973

👉 *Manet died in 1883. In 1886 a great exhibition was organized by Durand-Ruel in New York, which established the Impressionists in the United States. The members of the group set out in different directions during the following decades. Monet moved to Giverny where he painted his series of Waterlilies. Renoir studied Italian art and returned to painting with more emphasis on drawing. For a while, Pissarro was a follower of Neo-Impressionism. Cézanne moved away from Impressionist criteria. Degas, almost blind, took to sculpture. It was as the group was disbanding that Impressionism gained resounding recognition. In 1907, Manet's* Olympia *entered the Louvre, which also acquired Caillebotte's collection. All the main members of the movement died between 1894 and 1927: Caillebotte in 1894, Morisot in 1895, Sisley in 1899, Pissarro in 1903, Cézanne in 1906, Degas in 1917, Renoir in 1919, Monet and Cassatt in 1926, Guillaumin in 1927. The chapter involving the group that revolutionized modern art had come to a close.*

♦ DELACROIX
Liberty Leading the People, a symbolic view of the French revolution of 1830, a famous work by Eugène Delacroix, one of the early nineteenth-century French masters. Delacroix was the main artist at the 1855 Universal Exposition, exhibiting thirty-five paintings and acclaimed by, among others, the poet Baudelaire.

♦ MONET
In 1873, Impressionist painting was well-established and had acquired a style of its own. By comparison with earlier examples, Monet's *The Artist's House at Argenteuil* was a completely new type of painting, an example of the art that was breaking all ties with academic teaching and paving the way for the evolution of modern art.

♦ SEURAT
Sunday Afternoon on the Island of La Grande Jatte (1886) by Georges Seurat (1851-1891) is an example of "Neo-Impressionist" style. With Paul Signac (1863-1935), Seurat tried to give a scientific basis to Impressionism by using a technique based on very small, uniform, pointed brushstrokes.

♦ MATISSE
During the first years of the twentieth century, Henri Matisse (1869-1959) was a leading figure in a movement called "Fauvism", which took Impressionist studies to the extreme by eliminating everything that was not color from the canvas. *Luxe, Calme et Volupté* (1904-5) is a painting made up only of brushstrokes.

♦ INGRES AND CABANEL

Jean Auguste Dominique Ingres was a rival of Delacroix. (Left) *Le Bain Turc (Turkish Bath)*, 1862, is an example of his art that influenced Degas. Alexandre Cabanel was a traditional painter. *The Birth of Venus* (right), a dull and conventional work painted in 1863, was acquired by Napoleon III.

♦ GAUGUIN

Paul Gauguin (1848-1903) exhibited with the Impressionists and assimilated their style before developing his own distinctive manner and concentrating on the portrayal of distant, Polynesian countries. Eventually he left Paris, to live in Polynesia. *The Beach at Dieppe*, painted in 1885, is an early work in Impressionist style.

♦ TOULOUSE-LAUTREC

He was famous for his graphic art portraying the world of cafés and nightclubs. He might not have turned to painting if he had not learned from the Impressionists, especially Degas whom Toulouse-Lautrec (1864-1901) greatly admired. *At the Moulin Rouge*, painted in 1892, is one of his best-known works.

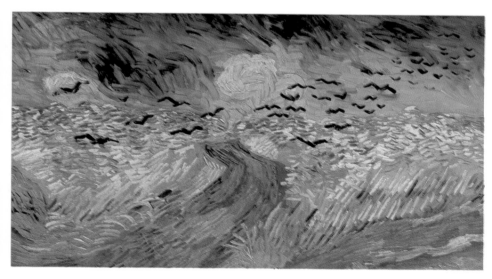

♦ VAN GOGH AND MUNCH

The art of Vincent van Gogh (1853-1890) does not belong to any school, although Impressionism is the starting point. *Wheatfield with Crows* (1890, left) was his last work. Edvard Munch (1863-1944), who became an Expressionist, was initially influenced by Pissarro and Monet, as can be seen in *Rue Lafayette* (1891, right).

♦ CÉZANNE

Late in life, Cézanne painted a series of landscapes that seemed to pave the way for a great twentieth-century painting movement, Cubism. *House on a Hill* (1904-6) is an example. The brushstrokes, all made with geometric precision, seem to "construct" the subject of the painting instead of depicting it.

♦ PICASSO

Cubism was begun with *Les Demoiselles d'Avignon*, painted in 1907 by Pablo Picasso. Cézanne was the last link with the Impressionist style and the admiration Picasso had for him is obvious. Twentieth-century art, for which the Impressionist painters had prepared the way, was to follow a different route.

EDOUARD MANET

Manet's most famous painting, *Le Déjeuner sur l'herbe*, shows this painter's uniqueness compared both to the academic artists, who hated him, and to the Impressionist painters themselves, who considered him a master even though he never actively took part in the group. From the point of view of composition and drawing, the painting respects all the traditional rules. Its inspiration was, in fact, a sixteenth-century work. From the point of view of painting technique, the picture makes use of the innovations introduced by Realist painters, who were respected if not liked. The subject, a naked woman seated with men dressed in contemporary clothes, provoked a scandalized response.

♦ His life
Edouard Manet was born in Paris in 1832, to a well-off family. When he was eighteen, he entered the atelier of Thomas Couture, but very soon took up his own personal research, studying closely the works of Italian and Spanish artists in the Louvre collection. *Le Déjeuner sur l'herbe*, painted in 1863, was the first of his "scandalous" works, followed in 1865 by *Olympia*. His contempt for

traditional painting earned him the respect of all the Impressionists. However, Manet did not join the group and did not take part in any of their exhibitions. From 1868 onwards he exhibited regularly at the Salon, which he considered to be "the real battleground" for the new art. In later years he widened the range of his subjects with portraits and still life. He died in 1883 as a result of an infection in his leg, from which he had suffered since 1876.

♦ With Mallarmé Manet (right) with Méry Laurent and   Mallarmé, photographed in 1872.

Many of the figures in Le Déjeuner sur l'herbe, *and some of their poses, place Manet within the Impressionist group, even though, for other reasons, he remained apart from this artistic movement. Unlike Monet or Renoir, he continued to place considerable importance on drawing. Until he*

began to paint "en plein air", the construction of his paintings was very carefully thought out. However, in his later years, Manet associated himself closely with Impressionist techniques. He quite often used the "en plein air" method and painted in a more free and spontaneous way.

♦ The inspiration
The Judgement of Paris by Marcantonio Raimondi (after   Raphael), c. 1515, was the work that inspired *Le Déjeuner.*

♦ LANDSCAPES
The way the trees on the right of the canvas are painted is reminiscent of the "Barbizon school", the group of landscape artists who were the first to use the "en plein air" painting technique.

♦ A SCANDALOUS SUBJECT
In *The Absinthe Drinker*, painted in 1859, Manet depicts an alcoholic. The work was rejected by the Salon jury.

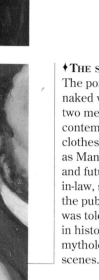

♦ THE SUBJECT
The portrayal of a naked woman with two men dressed in contemporary clothes, recognized as Manet's brother and future brother-in-law, scandalized the public. The nude was tolerated only in historical or mythological scenes.

♦ AT THE TUILERIES
In 1862 Manet painted *Music in the Tuileries Gardens*, one of the first portrayals of the lively, fashionable atmosphere of an open-air concert.

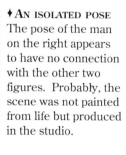

♦ AN ISOLATED POSE
The pose of the man on the right appears to have no connection with the other two figures. Probably, the scene was not painted from life but produced in the studio.

THE CORRIDA ♦
Mlle Victorine in the Costume of an Espada, painted in 1862. Manet shows his interest in the world of bullfighting.

AMERICAN WAR ♦
An episode from the American Civil War, *The Battle of the Kearsage and the Alabama* (fought outside Cherbourg), painted in 1864.

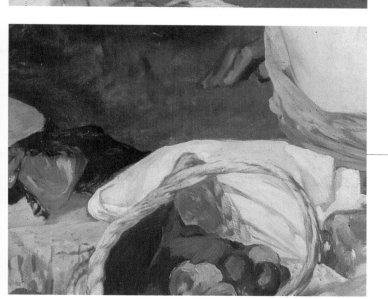

♦ STILL LIFE
The basket of fruit in the left foreground of *Le Déjeuner*, a homage to still life art of previous centuries, shows Manet's link with painting of the past.

CLAUDE MONET

A simple composition which can be divided horizontally into three areas: the sky, the countryside bordered by a clump of trees, the field in the foreground. Two haystacks, a common feature of country landscapes, stand in the center of the painting. For Monet, these were only a pretext for depicting the effects of the light. To do so, he used a series of close-set, many-colored brushstrokes: blue, white, various tones of red and violet. The end result is that the haystacks appear as two luminous objects which, for the person looking at the painting, have picked up the sunlight.

♦ **WATERLILIES**
Monet in Giverny painting one of his great canvases dedicated to waterlilies.

♦ HIS LIFE

Born in Paris in 1840, Claude Monet lived in Le Havre from 1845 to 1858. In 1859 he returned to the capital where he attended courses at the Académie Suisse. During the 1860s he concentrated on painting "en plein air", with Bazille, Renoir and Sisley. He met Manet and took part in Parisian cultural life. In 1870, mid-war, he took shelter in London where he met the art

dealer Paul Durand-Ruel. He returned to France in 1871, after a brief period in Holland, and took up residence in Argenteuil. In 1874 he took part in the group's first exhibition. In 1883 he moved to Giverny, a town on the Seine to the north of Paris, where he worked on his series. In 1886 Durand-Ruel organized an exhibition in New York. In 1889 Monet exhibited successfully at Petit's Paris gallery. He bought his house in Giverny in 1890 and lived there until his death in 1926, continuing to paint despite serious problems with his sight.

There are two reasons why Monet has been called "the most impressionistic of the Impressionists": his never-ending love for open scenery, parks, gardens and sun-drenched countryside, and the precision with which he conducted his painting studies, aiming to portray shimmering light and the variable color of things. The canvases dedicated to Rouen Cathedral (page 42) are the most significant testimony to his

perseverance. His consistency placed him at the forefront of the Impressionist group. "Forget what you see before your eyes," he once said, "a tree, a house, a field, and simply think: here there's a small blue square, there a pink rectangle, there a yellow streak, and paint what appears before you."

♦ **OLD AGE**
Monet in his Giverny studio, photographed at the beginning of the twentieth century.

VÉTHEUIL IN SUMMER ♦
Monet spent from 1878 to 1881 in Vétheuil, a small town on the Seine, north of Paris. Here he painted various views, in all seasons.

BORDIGHERA ♦
At the end of 1883 Monet took a trip to the Ligurian (Italian) riviera. *Lemon Trees at Bordighera* is one of his works from this period.

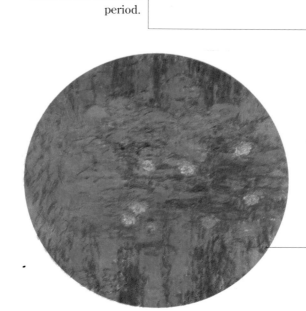

♦ LIGHTING
To achieve the lighting effect on the larger of the two haystacks, Monet used very thick brushstrokes ranging from red through orange to pink, with small, blue strokes and very bright touches of white. The trees and the countryside are composed of blues and greens, almost indistinguishable at close range.

♦ LILY POND
The waterlilies in his pond at Giverny provided Monet with an unending source of inspiration.

♦ BOAT-RACES
Regatta at Argenteuil, painted in 1872, is one of the first examples of Monet's interest in the variety of color that can be seen in water.

VÉTHEUIL IN WINTER ♦
In this winter scene of Vétheuil, Monet used pale tones for the snow, and dark, cold colors to depict the Seine, almost frozen.

PIERRE AUGUSTE RENOIR

The Moulin de la Galette was a dance hall located in rue Lepic in the Montmartre district. During the afternoons of public holidays it would be full of people dancing, talking and drinking. The atmosphere was happy and carefree. Renoir took a canvas to the Moulin and painted his surroundings. Later, in his studio, he finished the work. He used small, bright and colorful brushstrokes, played with the lighting effect created by the leaves on the trees and arranged the figures loosely. In one "snapshot", full of vitality and color, he portrayed all the bustle and perfume of Parisian entertainment. It was because of works like this that Renoir was called "the painter of happiness".

♦ **THE BATHERS**
Painted in 1918-19, this was Renoir's last work. It is a daring painting, made up of stark contrasts, and very different from his early work. *The Great Bathers* (below), with its clearly defined setting, was painted in the studio in 1884-87. In this work, Renoir has moved away from the Impressionist technique.

From a technical point of view, Renoir and Monet painted in very similar ways. There was good reason for them to compete on the same subjects (for example, La Grenouillère, page 28). It was a sort of friendly challenge. Renoir's painting, more than Monet's, seems to be the result of the pleasure he took in improvisation and has a freshness beyond compare. However, we should not be fooled by this. It is only seemingly spontaneous, and the "freshness" of his paintings was, in truth, the result of serious thought and accurate study.

♦ IN ARGENTEUIL
Sailboats at Argenteuil, painted by Renoir in 1874, shows Monet's influence. Monet was inspired by the same subject.

♦ PART OF A LARGER SCENE
Placing figures right at the edge of the painting gives the impression that the scene carries on beyond the canvas.

♦ SHOWING MOVEMENT
Using reflections and shade and the effects of pale and dark colors, Renoir depicts movement of the figures in the background.

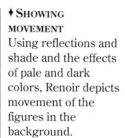

♦ THE GARDEN
During the time when he was painting the Moulin de la Galette in Montmartre, Renoir rented an apartment-studio. In this work, *The Garden of the Rue Cortot*, he depicts the colors and fresh atmosphere of its large, untended garden. Every day his friends helped him carry the canvas of *Le Moulin de la Galette* into the garden, where he concentrated on putting the finishing touches to the painting.

♦ ARAB FESTIVAL
In 1881 Renoir went to North Africa for a month, painting scenes of the lives of the local population with great freedom of expression. In this work, white brushstrokes are used to give a sense of the African heat.

EDGAR DEGAS

The theater was a main source of entertainment for Parisians during the second half of the nineteenth century. The atmosphere of first nights at the Opéra, of concerts and the ballet was reproduced in many Impressionist paintings. But Degas was also interested in what went on behind the scenes, before a performance. Rehearsals were far less happy events, without the excitement of an opening night. In *The Rehearsal on Stage* he captures the repetitious nature of a job like any other: the ballerinas' movements, rehearsed and re-rehearsed, an old teacher, two bored onlookers. The drawing is precise and defined, but the painting was completed in the studio. "Copying what we see is all very well," Degas said, "but it is much better to draw what we remember."

♦ HIS LIFE
Born in Paris in 1843, a law graduate, Edgar Degas began his artistic apprenticeship in Barrias' studio and at the Louvre. In 1855 he met Ingres, whom he greatly admired. Between 1856 and 1859 he often travelled to Italy, visiting Rome, Florence and Naples. In 1859 he returned to Paris, met Manet, became a regular member of the meetings at the Café Guerbois and exhibited at the Salon. During the Franco-Prussian war he enrolled in the National Guard. When he returned to Paris in 1873, after a trip to New Orleans, he once more contacted the Impressionists and took part in almost all of the group's exhibitions. He was one of the artists most inspired by photographic techniques and by Japanese art. During the 1880s he admired Gauguin's work and travelled to Spain and Morocco. In 1893 his first and only personal exhibition was held in Durand-Ruel's gallery. At the close of the century, almost blind, he also dedicated himself to sculpture. He died in September 1917.

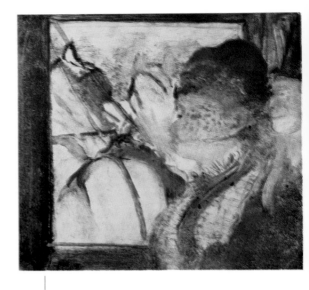

♦ IN THE OMNIBUS
A glimpse of everyday life: a man and woman in a tramcar, a spontaneous view like a snapshot.

"What I do is the result of thought and study....I know nothing about inspiration, spontaneity and feeling." This statement helps us to understand Degas' unique personality. Unlike most of the Impressionists, he worked only in the studio, often from memory. He was not very interested in nature, and he held drawing in great respect. He did, however, share the others' interest in modern life and, like them, had an exceptional talent for experimentation. Degas explored all aspects of photography and invented new painting techniques. Moments are captured in his paintings, like film frames.*

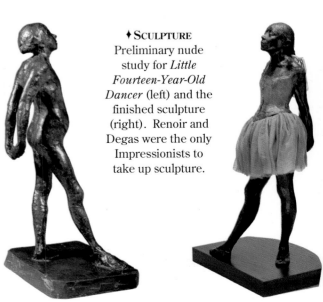

♦ SCULPTURE
Preliminary nude study for *Little Fourteen-Year-Old Dancer* (left) and the finished sculpture (right). Renoir and Degas were the only Impressionists to take up sculpture.

♦ **BALLERINAS**
Degas showed his talent for drawing in the way he sketched ballerinas. Before beginning the painting, he made a series of preparatory drawings, studying the dancers' positions and movements and the contours of their limbs.

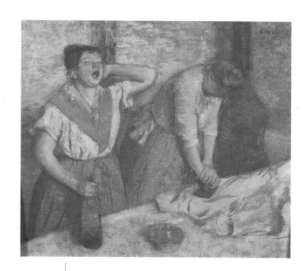

♦ **WOMEN IRONING**
Although an aristocrat, Degas was always interested in the fatigue of

women's work. *Women Ironing*, 1884-86, is one of his many paintings on the subject.

♦ **IN THE BACKGROUND**
These two men - particularly the figure on the right with his hands in his pockets and his legs crossed - have the appearance of onlookers bored with the dancers' routines.

♦ **NUDES**
Getting out of the Bath . "To date, the nude has always been presented in poses meant for public viewing. My women, on the other hand, are simple, honest people, only intent on taking care of their own bodies."

♦ **WEARINESS**
A yawning ballerina at a moment of rest, expresses the weariness and boredom of monotonous work.

♦ **ABSINTHE**
In *Absinthe*, Degas portrays two examples of human degradation: a Bohemian and a prostitute destroyed by alcohol. The

image is cut to highlight the empty tables. Degas chose only a limited range of colors, black, ochre and white, to describe the squalor of the scene.

♦ **THE MASTER**
To give a sense of movement to the scene, Degas used the figure of the master, painted in dark colors, to separate the two main parts of the painting - the ballerinas rehearsing on the right and those resting on the left.

PAUL CÉZANNE

Paul Cézanne was born in Aix-en-Provence in 1839, to a well-off family. Having moved to Paris in 1861, he exhibited without success at the Salon des Refusés in 1863 and his works were regularly rejected by the official Salon. He made contact with the Impressionists, began to paint "en plein air", and took part in two of the movement's exhibitions, in 1874 and 1877. He then went to live in Provence. He did not exhibit again for about twenty years, but widened his knowledge of art through personal, isolated study carried out with the patience of a craftsman. Towards the close of the century he reaped the benefits of his hard work. His personal exhibition in 1895 was a great success. He took part in the Salon des Indépendants in 1899, 1900 and 1902 and became established at the 1904 Salon d'Autômne. Like other Impressionist painters, he often returned to the same subject. In later years, a diabetic, he withdrew to Aix where he worked on *The Large Bathers*, an ambitious work preceded by ten years of study. He died in 1906.

In order to paint this view of Mont Sainte-Victoire in Provence, Cézanne worked in an abandoned quarry cluttered with piles of rocks and far away from the subject of the picture. The painting has four elements: the rocks in the foreground, the trees, the sky and the distant outline of the mountain. They are distinctly separate, but by means of even, geometric brushstrokes and the effect of color, Cézanne manages to unify them and creates the feeling that a profound order exists in nature, described better by painting than any other art form.

♦ **THE SAME SUBJECT** Above and below, two of the many other canvases Cézanne painted of the Sainte-Victoire mountain.

Cézanne's development was probably the most original. Because of his interest in nature, he used many of the group's "discoveries", including the "en plein air" method of painting and "brushstroke" technique, but with different results, especially in his later works. While most of the Impressionists achieved an improvised effect, Cézanne sought something more "durable". He developed a diagonal surface patterning of small, separate, parallel strokes. The objects he depicted - stones, leaves, houses - became geometric shapes. Soon afterwards, Cubist painters would develop these studies.

♦ THE SUMMIT
The bulk of the mountain, which seems to rise straight out of the quarry, was achieved mainly with vertical, grey strokes that gradually shade off until reaching the sky.

♦ BATHERS
The Large Bathers, painted between 1898 and 1905, and Cézanne's largest canvas, is the work which took him the longest time to complete. In bathers, the theme of many paintings, Cézanne saw a perfect union between humans and nature.

♦ ROCKS
These are in the foreground, painted in ochre, but seem to belong to the same plane as the mountain, even though they are very distant from it. Cézanne used neat and geometric brush-strokes to paint them.

THE CARD PLAYERS ♦
Two men at a card table in a bare and poor-looking room, concentrating on the cards, absorbed in a seemingly ritual game that takes place every day.

♦ TREES
The brushstrokes are much closer together and more blurred in the painting of the clump of trees on the left of the work, but there is still some uniformity in their diagonal direction. All the elements making up the scene are closely related so that, at first sight, the painting looks like a sculpture without depth.

♦ APPLES
Cézanne was a great still life painter and had a special preference for apples in his still life work. The appeal of this ordinary fruit was its simplicity and perfect shape. He saw everything in terms of its geometric shape and used the apple to practice continually on the spherical form.

CAMILLE PISSARRO

This canvas, *The Backwoods at l'Hermitage*, shows the degree of refinement an Impressionist artist could achieve when painting a landscape. Everything is shrouded in the shade created by the trees, and the two figures in the center, a goat and a man lying down, can hardly be seen. With brushstrokes that are at times tiny - for the leaves - and at times much longer - for the tree-trunks - and by using the light originating from the white house in the background, Pissarro was able to represent the tones of color and the variety of light found in a wood.

♦ FACTORY NEAR PONTOISE
Pissarro combined a river landscape with factory chimneys in this work.

♦ HIS LIFE
Born in Saint-Thomas in the Antilles in 1830, Pissarro settled in Paris in 1855. At first he was greatly influenced by the painting and social-mindedness of Millet, as well as by the work of Corot and Daubigny. He soon broke away from the academics and exhibited at the Salon des Refusés in 1863. In 1870, while France was involved in the disastrous war with Prussia, Pissarro was with Monet in London. It was during this stay in the English capital that they met the art dealer Paul Durand-Ruel. Having returned to France in 1871, Pissarro worked in Pontoise and Eragny. After 1885 he took an interest in the Neo-Impressionist theories of Seurat and Signac, but his enthusiasm for their style did not last long and in the 1890s he returned to a less restrained style of painting. He died in November 1903.

Camille Pissarro could be described as the father of the Impressionist movement. He was the only group member not to miss any of the movement's exhibitions; he was the most open and humane of them all; he was the one to whom the younger painters turned for advice and lessons. He had a strong influence over his younger companions. He was the first of the painters to stop using bitumen, black and sienna on the palette, thus changing the color range to much lighter shades. In his decidedly Impressionist works, he managed to combine a lively sense of color with a general balance of composition.

♦ SIMPLE PEOPLE
Young Woman Washing Dishes, 1882, marked a return of Pissarro's interest in poor, country folk, portrayed with simplicity. The painting is part of a series of thirty works which Pissarro showed at the 1882 exhibition.

ALFRED SISLEY

In *Boats on the Seine*, a work completed all in one sitting, Sisley used a few basic colors - mainly green and blue - to depict a common scene: large boats on the river, busy people along the banks on a cloudy day. He used the same colors for the sky as for the water. The differences between the two planes of the painting result from the different directions of the brushstrokes: horizontal as far as the line of houses, diagonal or intricate for the sky, to mix and blend the color.

♦ HIS LIFE
The son of a wealthy English merchant who settled in France, Sisley was born in Paris in 1839. From 1861 he attended the Ecole des Beaux-Arts and then the atelier of Charles Gleyre, where he remained until 1864, becoming friendly with Monet, Renoir and Bazille. He was part of the

Café Guerbois group. During the Franco-Prussian war he took shelter in Louveciennes. In 1871 his father went bankrupt, became ill and very soon died, leaving Sisley in disastrous financial straits. In 1872 Monet and Pissarro introduced him to the art dealer Paul Durand-Ruel, who immediately bought some of his paintings. He then took part in the Impressionist exhibitions of 1874, 1876, 1877 and 1882. Late in life he isolated himself in Moret-sur-Loing, where he died in poverty in 1899.

♦ SCENE OF DISASTER In 1876 the Seine overflowed its banks at Marly-le-Roi. In *Floods at Port-Marly*, Sisley expresses the desolation after the disaster.

Sisley was above all a landscape painter. He painted many scenes of his favorite places, the French country towns around Paris, and showed no interest in portraying city life. Like Monet, he was spurred on by his great love of nature. Above all, he was fascinated by water, river life and the silent depth of the sky. His works, which always show great knowledge of the use of color, often contain elements of tenderness and softness that set him apart and show him to have been a refined and sensitive artist even if lacking the talent for innovation displayed by other members of the group.

♦ LOUVECIENNES *Rue de la Machine*: a winter scene, a sweeping view and a vast sky giving depth to the painting.

BERTHE MORISOT

Two women, mother and daughter, one dressed in black and the other in white, sitting in their middle-class home. The artist's mother and sister, Edma, posed for this painting. Berthe Morisot shows her talent as a portrait painter and her sensitivity when portraying sad situations such as this: two women unable to communicate, each enclosed by her own solitude.

✦ HARBOR OF LORIENT Berthe's sister Edma posed for this painting with its bright and delicate tones.

✦ HER LIFE
Born in Bourges in 1841, Berthe Morisot studied with Guichard in Paris and, from 1862 to 1868, was one of Corot's students together with her sister Edma. Until 1873 she was regularly admitted to the Salon. After this date, and above all because of the influence of Manet whom she met in 1868 and for whom she posed, she changed direction to a decidedly Impressionist style. She may or may not have been in love with Manet, but their relationship always remained one of mutual respect. She married Manet's brother, Eugène, in 1874, and died in Paris in 1895.

✦ PAINTED BY MANET
Morisot had a long-standing relationship with Manet, who painted this portrait of her. Manet admired her and gave her a great deal of advice, occasionally intervening in her work.

✦ LA TOILETTE
Indoor Parisian scenes and portraits of women talking or, as in this case, beautifying themselves are some of the subjects typical of Morisot's painting.

✦ QUAY AT BOUGIVAL
Painted in 1883, the setting is a town by the Seine, not far from Paris. The picture is dominated by one tone that merges the river, its banks and the sky into one.

Berthe Morisot had a style based on the use of pale colors which was to influence Manet himself. She took part in almost all of the Impressionist movement's exhibitions. Her favorite subjects were water, landscapes and family scenes, always captured with spontaneity. Late in life, she used more decisive brushstrokes and her painting showed greater consistency, but Morisot never lost the refinement that was typical of her sensitivity as a cultured and kindly woman.

MARY CASSATT

Mary Cassatt made close studies of the theater, one of the places where the bourgeoisie liked to go for entertainment. *Woman in Black at the Opéra* is the masterpiece in a series of works dedicated to the subject, and was also the first painting of its kind to focus attention on the audience. By observing the atmosphere inside a theater box, Cassatt depicts the theater not only as a place where performances are held but also, and above all perhaps, as a setting for a fashionable and social occasion.

♦ **HER LIFE**
Born in the United States, in Pittsburgh, in 1845, Mary Cassatt went to Paris in 1866. She already had an academic training, having attended the Pennsylvania Academy of Fine Art. She exhibited at the 1868 Salon. After the war of 1870 she travelled a great deal, visiting Antwerp, Rome and Seville. When she returned to Paris, she became friendly with Degas who introduced her into the Impressionist group. A friend of Berthe Morisot and Mallarmé, she took part in all the Impressionist exhibitions from 1879, except for that of 1882. In 1894 she took up residence in Beaufresné castle, north-west of Paris. She died in 1926.

♦ **THE BATH**
Children always interested Cassatt as subjects because of their spontaneity. This work, painted in 1892, is accurately drawn and delicately colored.

♦ **IN THE OMNIBUS**
Two women and a little girl in a drawing that shows Cassatt's interest in Japanese art.

♦ **PAINTED BY DEGAS**
Mary Cassatt in a portrait by Degas who "discovered" her and introduced her into the circle of Parisian painters.

In addition to her pictures of the theater, Mary Cassatt is known for her drawings and etchings which show her refined sensibility and great attention to lessons learned from Japanese art. She explored the middle-class home, portraying scenes of family life and painting women and children. Like Degas, who introduced her into the Impressionist group, Cassatt considered composition to be of great importance and was not very interested in landscape painting.

A STUDY ♦
There is a strange story attached to this work. It began with a bet with Degas that style could be found even in a vulgar-looking a model. Degas lost the bet and praised Cassatt's painting.

ARMAND GUILLAUMIN

Against the background of an industrial landscape seen at night, along the banks of the Seine, while work continues and a chimney is still burning, a few men - almost camouflaged by the dark colors of the ground and the shade of the trees and factories - earn a living not by working, but by stealing. *Quai de Bercy* is a painting that summarizes the art of Armand Guillaumin: decisive colors and a personal interest in socially related subjects and in representing the squalid, urban life created by industrial development.

♦ HIS LIFE
Born in Paris in 1841, before turning to art Guillaumin did menial jobs: for a few years he was a garbage collector. A lottery win freed him to take up painting. He soon came into contact with Cézanne and Pissarro, with whom he painted in Pontoise and Auvers. He took part in the first Impressionist exhibition and in almost all the others. His work was also shown at the great exhibition organized by Durand-Ruel in New York in 1886. He died in Orly in 1927, his later works demonstrating his alliance with new trends in French painting, like Fauvism.

♦ SUNSET AT IVRY
A suburban scene, the red light of sunset streaked with smoke from a chimney stack; no human presence. With this work, painted in 1873, Guillaumin displayed his interest in the less "beautiful" aspects of industrial life.

♦ SELF-PORTRAIT
Guillaumin in a self-portait of 1878. He lived longer than any of the other Impressionists, surviving Monet and Cassatt. He was not much admired during his lifetime. His art has now been rediscovered.

The art of Armand Guillaumin is characterized by clarity and vivid color; he showed little interest in shaded tones. His paintings often had an energy that was unusual for the Impressionist group. On the other hand, they lacked the richness of shading and the light touch of artists like Monet or Renoir. Guillaumin was to have considerable influence on the generation of painters who followed the Impressionists. His interest in the people and places of industrial society was new to French art. Guillaumin was the first painter regularly to depict the outskirts of cities.

♦ THE SEINE AT PARIS
This work, painted in 1871, with its compact, dark colors, was exhibited at the Impressionists' third show, in 1877.

GUSTAVE CAILLEBOTTE

Inside a middle-class Parisian house, three workers are planing the wooden floor. Caillebotte was very precise in his portrayal of their work. The man on the right is levelling the edges of the planks, the man in the middle is planing off the surface of the floor, the man on the left is picking up a file to sharpen the planing blade. Their faces are expressionless because of the repetitive nature of their work. The choice of subject was considered an insult to painting. But supporters of Caillebotte praised the innovative nature of *The Floorscrapers*.

♦ ROOFTOPS UNDER THE SNOW
A view over Parisian houses after a snowfall, depicted by Caillebotte with the precision of a Realist painter.

♦ HIS LIFE
Born in Paris in 1848, in 1873 Caillebotte met Monet who "discovered" him and asked him to take part in the Impressionists' first exhibition, in 1874. He not only took part in five of the group's exhibitions but organized and financed some of them, beginning with the second in 1876. His painting was ultra-modern, although his original Realist style is evident. He died in 1894, leaving his collection of sixty-seven works by the greatest Impressionist painters to the state, on condition that they be exhibited at the Louvre. This did not happen, however, until 1937.

♦ MONET RESTING
Caillebotte had a sincere affection for Claude Monet. The subject of this canvas is his friend the painter, whom he depicts resting during a trip to the country.

Caillebotte was a painter of Parisian scenes and used bold, cut-away views as in photography: glistening rain-drenched streets with people promenading, views of the boulevards and the new bridges over the Seine. In his most successful paintings, the brushstrokes are so clearly defined that some did not consider him an Impressionist. He was a Realist who, instead of the workers and peasants of earlier times, treated contemporary Parisian society. His paintings show people going about their normal business on the Pont de l'Europe or glimpses of Haussmann's great boulevards. His art combined real-life detail with the sense of color he perceived in people on the streets.

♦ BOATING
Caillebotte loved rowing. He was an engineer, who specialized in ship-building, and painted in his free time. Monet met him at Argenteuil and possibly asked him to help build his studio-boat.

◆ KEY DATES

1855	First Universal Exposition in Paris, at the Palais de l'Industrie. Camille Pissarro moves from the Virgin Islands to the French capital.
1863	Salon des Refusés, with works by Manet, Pissarro, Guillaumin and Cézanne. Death of Delacroix. Monet works "en plein air" in the Forest of Fontainebleau.
1865	Manet shocks the Salon with *Olympia*. Renoir and Sisley work "en plein air" in the Forest of Fontainebleau.
1867	The year of the Paris Universal Exposition where Manet, Courbet and Renoir have personal pavilions. Deaths of Ingres and Baudelaire.
1869	The group begins to meet in the Batignolles district, at the Café Guerbois. Monet and Renoir paint at La Grenouillère.
1870	On July 18 war breaks out between France and Prussia. On September 2 the French troops are defeated at Sedan. On September 4 the Third Republic is proclaimed.
1871	On January 28 the armistice between France and Prussia is signed. Between March 18 and May 28 the Paris Commune is proclaimed. Courbet is arrested.
1872	The art dealer Paul Durand-Ruel, who has met Monet and Pissarro in London, is introduced to Manet, Degas and Sisley.
1873	Death of Napoleon III. Courbet flees to Switzerland. Durand-Ruel exhibits the Impressionists' works in London. Monet forms a close friendship with Caillebotte.
1874	First joint Impressionist exhibition in Nadar's studio. Manet and Mary Cassatt do not take part but exhibit at the Salon.
1875	The paintings not sold at the 1874 exhibition are auctioned, at very low prices, at the Hôtel Drouot. Deaths of Millet and Corot.
1878	Durand-Ruel exhibits 300 works by painters of the Barbizon School at the Paris Universal Exposition. Manet shows the first symptoms of his illness.
1881	The Salon is no longer controlled by the state. Manet is proposed for the Legion of Honor. Renoir travels to Africa and Italy.
1882	A great retrospective exhibition of Courbet is held in Paris. Petit, the dealer and rival of Durand-Ruel, founds the International Exposition.
1883	Impressionist exhibition organized by Durand-Ruel in London, Berlin, Rotterdam. The Impressionists are also exhibited in New York and Boston. Death of Manet.
1884	Commemorative exhibition of Manet at the Ecole des Beaux-Arts. Cézanne, with other artists, founds the Société des Indépendants.
1885	Death of Victor Hugo. Pissarro meets Seurat and Signac. Monet takes part in Petit's fourth International Exposition. Sisley is in dire financial straits.
1886	The Impressionist group's eighth and last joint exhibition. Durand-Ruel exhibits Impressionist works in the United States. The group disbands. Each painter now follows a personal line of study.

◆ MUSEUMS AND GALLERIES

The story of the museums that have collected works by the Impressionist painters runs along with the history of the group and its success on the international market. Obviously, the most important collections are found in France, but many British and American museums also hold some of the movement's masterpieces. This is a result of the work of the first art dealers, especially Paul Durand-Ruel, who promoted Impressionist paintings. The following are the main museums housing Impressionist works.

FRANCE

MUSÉE MARMOTTAN, PARIS
It contains some of the fundamental works of Impressionism, like *Impression: Sunrise* by Monet, which gave the movement its name.

MUSÉE D'ORSAY, PARIS
The museum, originally the Orsay railway station, is an example of the reconstruction of civic buildings as museums. The station was opened on July 14, 1900. It was adapted into a museum by a group of French architects (Renaud Bardon, Pierre Colboc, Jean-Paul Philippon) and by the Italian architect Gae Aulenti. The Musée d'Orsay, opened in 1988, is the great gallery of nineteenth-century French art. It also houses the most important Romantic and Realist paintings and contains the most outstanding collection of Impressionist paintings in the world, including *Olympia* and *Le Déjeuner sur l'herbe* by Manet, *Regatta at Argenteuil* by Monet, *The Star* by Degas, *Le Moulin Rouge* by Renoir, *The Card Players* by Cézanne, *The Floorscrapers* by Caillebotte.

GREAT BRITAIN

COURTAULD INSTITUTE GALLERIES, LONDON
Many works by French and European Impressionist and Post-Impressionist artists including Cézanne and Gauguin, Manet (*A Bar at the Folies-Bergère*) and Monet, Van Gogh and Renoir (*The Box at the Opéra*).

FITZWILLIAM MUSEUM, CAMBRIDGE
Contains works by Italian masters, Impressionists (*Gust of Wind* by Renoir) and English painters.

GLASGOW ART GALLERY AND MUSEUM
Impressionism is particularly well represented.

THE NATIONAL GALLERY, LONDON
Has some very famous Impressionist works, including Manet's *Execution of Maximilian*, Monet's *Waterlilies* and Renoir' *Umbrellas*.

THE NATIONAL MUSEUM OF WALES, CARDIFF
Houses works by English and Welsh painters and also has a collection of Impressionist paintings (Pissarro, *Boulevard Montmartre, Night Effect*).

UNITED STATES

MUSEUM OF FINE ARTS, BOSTON
Founded in 1870, it is divided into various sections including Asian art and classical Greek and Roman art, Egyptian art and Italian and Flemish art. It houses many Romantic and Impressionist French works: Delacroix, Corot, Millet, Gauguin, Degas (*Carriage at the Races*), Cézanne, Manet, Renoir, Cassatt (*Woman in Black at the Opéra*).

THE ART INSTITUTE OF CHICAGO
The museum contains works from all eras, from Italian masters to contemporary painters. Its collection of French paintings from the Impressionist and Post-Impressionist period is one of the most important in the world (Caillebotte, *Paris, A Rainy Day*; Manet, *Horse-Racing at Longchamps*; Seurat, *Sunday Afternoon on the Island of La Grande Jatte*).

PHILADELPHIA MUSEUM OF ART
Founded in 1875 and located in a large, temple-like building in Fairmount Park, the museum has Italian and Flemish works and many Impressionist paintings (Cézanne, *The Large Bathers*).

THE METROPOLITAN MUSEUM OF ART, NEW YORK
Founded in 1870, it houses a very valuable collection, today numbering 3 million pieces. It has works from all periods and all schools including a significant collection of Impressionist paintings (Monet, *La Grenouillère*).

MUSEUM OF MODERN ART, NEW YORK
The largest museum of modern art in the world, it houses works by the most important masters and from the various nineteenth- and twentieth-century artistic trends, ranging from Impressionism to German Expressionism, Cubism, Abstract art and up to the most recent movements.

THE NATIONAL GALLERY OF ART, WASHINGTON, D.C.
It is located in a building that was finished in the early 1940s. Its collections, made up of acquisitions and donations of public and private collections, include works by old European masters, paintings by eighteenth- and nineteenth-century French, American and European artists and many important Impressionist and Post-Impressionist works (Manet, *Masked Ball at the Opéra*; Renoir, *Pont Neuf*).

♦ INDEX OF WORKS

◆ INDEX

◆ CREDITS

The original and previously unpublished illustrations in this book may only be reproduced with the prior permission of Donati-Giudici Associati, who holds the copyright.

The illustrations are by: L.R. Galante (pages 4-5, 10-11, 12-13, 20-21, 22-23, 24-25, 28-29, 30-31, 40-41); Andrea Ricciardi (pages 6-7, 8-9, 16-17, 34-35); Claudia Saraceni (pages 14, 38).

All efforts have been made to trace the copyright-holders of the other illustrations in the book. If any omissions have been made, this will be corrected at reprint.

Thanks are due to the following for their permission to use illustrations: Allen Memorial Art Museum, Oberlin; Art Gallery of Ontario, Toronto; The Art Institute of Chicago; Bibliothèque Nationale, Paris; British Museum, London; Monsieur C. Bührle, Zurich; The Carnegie Museum of Art, Pittsburgh; Courtauld Institute Galleries, London; Fitzwilliam Museum, Cambridge; Fogg Art Museum, Cambridge, Mass., Harvard University; Folkwang Museum, Essen; Frick Collection, New York; Galerie Bayeler, Basel; Grenoble Museum; Calouste Gulbenkian Foundation, Lisbon; Haags Gemeentehaus, The Hague; Institute of Arts, Minneapolis; Kunsthalle, Hamburg; Kunsthaus, Zurich; Metropolitan Museum of Art, New York; Musée des Beaux-Arts, Lyon; Musée des Beaux-Arts, Pau; Musée des Beaux-Arts, Reims; Musée des Beaux-Arts, Rouen; Musée des Beaux-Arts, Tournai; Musée Carnavalet, Paris; Musée d'Orsay, Paris; Musée du Louvre, Paris; Musée du Petit Palais, Geneva; Musée du Petit Palais, Paris; Musée Marmottan, Paris; Musée Municipale A.G. Poulain, Vernon; Musée Picasso, Paris; Musée Pissarro, Pontoise; Museum and Art Gallery, Birmingham; Museum of Art, Baltimore; Museum of Art, Cleveland; Museum of Art, Portland; Museum of Fine Arts, Boston; Museum of Fine Arts, Houston; Museum of Fine Arts, Springfield; Museum of Modern Art, New York; Nasjonalgalleriet, Oslo; National Gallery, London; National Gallery of Art, Washington, D.C.; National Museum of Wales, Cardiff; National Museum Vincent Van Gogh, Amsterdam; The Nelson Atkins Museum of Art, Kansas City; Neue Pinakothek, Munich; Ny Carlsberg Glyptothek, Copenhagen; Philadelphia Museum of Art; Phillips Collection, Washington, D.C.; Pushkin Museum, Moscow; Rijksmuseum Kröller-Müller, Otterlo; Rijksmuseum voor Volkenkunde, Leiden; Rijksmuseum, Amsterdam; Shelburne Museum, Vermont; Smithsonian Institution, Washington, D.C.; Staatsgalerie, Stuttgart; Statens Konstmuseer, Stockholm; Sterling and Francine Clark Institute, Williamstown, Mass.; Szépmüveszeti Museum, Budapest; The Tate Gallery, London; Virginia Museum of Fine Arts, Richmond.
ARCHIVIO ALINARI/GIRAUDON: 3, 7, 9, 10, 28, 33, 40, 42, 45, 46, 50, 55, 56, 57, 60, 62, 67, 70, 77, 80, 81, 90, 92, 95, 97, 103, 104, 106, 107, 112, 113, 121, 122, 123, 126, 127, 133, 137, 148, 152, 155, 157, 163, 169, 170, 171, 176, 189, 190; BRIDGEMAN/ARTEPHOT: 119, 130, 185; PHOTO SCALA, FLORENCE: 4, 18, 19, 22, 27, 32, 34, 36, 39, 41, 53, 59, 61, 72, 73, 74, 76, 83, 84, 85, 89, 91, 96, 116, 132, 141, 146, 165, 167, 177, 179, 180, 183; © PHOTO R.M.N.: 31, 37, 48, 64, 140; PHOTO BASSET: 42; BILDARCHIV PREUSISCHER KULTURBESITZ, BERLIN, photo Jörg P. Anders: 168; 2 © 1994 AIC, oil on canvas, 81.5x101.6 cm; 8 © 1994 AIC, oil on canvas, 212.2x276.2 cm; 11 © 1994 AIC, oil on canvas; 12 WNG, 1994 Board of Trustees, oil on canvas, 75.1x62.5 cm; 13 © 1994 AIC, etching, 4.3x29.9 cm; 14 WNG, 1994 Board of Trustees, soft ground etching, drypoint and aquatint in color; 15 © 1994 NYM; 17 Courtesy BFA, oil on canvas, 80x64.8; 20 cm Presented by the US Government in memory of Charles A. Loeser, on loan to the WNG, tela, 65.8x81 cm; 21 Purchased: W.P. Wilatach Coll.; 29 WNG, 1994 Board of Trustees; oil on canvas, 81x100.5 cm; 38 Purchased: Estate of the Late George D. Widener; 44 Courtesy BFA, 1931 Purchase Fund, oil on canvas, 36.5x55.9 cm; 54 © 1994 NYM; 65 WNG, 1994 Board of Trustees, oil on canvas, 45.8x60.5 cm; 86 © 1994 AIC, oil on canvas, 43.9x84.5 cm; 87 © 1994 NYM; 88 WNG, 1994 Board of Trustees, oil on canvas, 59x72.5 cm; 98 © 1994 AIC, oil on canvas, 43.9x84.5 cm; 99 Purchased: The Kenneth A. and Helen Spencer Foundation Acquisition Fund, oil on canvas, 80.4x60.3 cm; 101 © 1994 MM; 102 © 1994 AIC, oil on canvas, 66.5x82.3 cm; 105 © 1994 NYM; 108 © 1994 AIC, oil on canvas, 89.9x101; 109 cm Courtesy BFA, 1951 Purchase Fund, oil on canvas, 231.6 x 142.3 cm; 114 © 1994 NYM; 117 © MM; 118 WNG, 1994 Board of Trustees, oil on canvas, 100,4x66; 125 cm Courtesy BFA, 1951 Purchase Fund, oil on canvas, 231.6x142.3 cm; 131 WNG, 1994 Board of Trustees, oil on canvas; 136 © 1994 NYM; 139 © THE FRICK COLL., New York; 142 WNG, 1994 Board of Trustees, oil on canvas, 101x81.8 cm; 144 WNG, 1994 Board of Trustees, oil on canvas; 145 © 1994 AIC, oil on canvas, 60.3x80.4 cm; 147 on canvas, 243.9x233.7 cm; 149 oil on canvas, 125.1x163.2 cm; 151 WNG, 1994 Board of Trustees, oil on canvas, 73.2x92.1 cm; 158 © 1994 NYM; 162 © 1994 NYM; 166 © THE PHILLIPS COLL., WASHINGTON DC; 172 Acquired through the generosity of Mrs Alan M. Scaife, oil on canvas, 151.8x97.5 cm; 182 WNG, 1994 Board of Trustees, oil on canvas, 75.3x93.7 cm; 186 © 1994 AIC, oil on canvas, 61.5x50.3 cm; 187 © 1994 AIC, oil on canvas, 123x141 cm; 191 © THE PHILLIPS COLL., WASHINGTON DC; 194 © 1994 NYM, oil on canvas, 123x141 cm.
The paintings of Edvard Munch, Henri Matisse and Pablo Picasso on pages 44-45 have been reproduced with the authorization of the Società italiana degli autori ed editori, which has agreed to deal with any concerns about rights.